POTS AND CONTAINERS

POTS AND CONTAINERS

A PRACTICAL GUIDE

Sue Spielberg

THE NATIONAL TRUST

Published in Great Britain in 1998
The National Trust (Enterprises) Ltd
36 Queen Anne's Gate
London SW1H 9AS

ISBN 0 7078 0283 0

Cataloguing in Publication Data is available from the
British Library.

The author and the publishers are grateful to Andrew Lawson
for permission to reproduce the photograph on p.8 and to Tony
Murdoch for the picture on p.13 (*right*). All other photographs
are from the National Trust Photographic Library and are by
the following photographers: Neil Campbell-Sharp: front cover,
14-15; Stephen Robson: half title page, frontispiece, 6, 12, 13 (*left*);
Andrew Lawson: 9, 10; Rupert Truman: 16 (*top*), back cover;
Mike Williams: 16 (*below*).

Line drawings by Jim Robins

Designed and Typeset in Palatino by the
Newton Engert Partnership

Printed in Great Britain by Butler & Tanner Limited

HALF TITLE: Wooden half-barrels hold exuberant bedding
displays at Tatton Park. This example is in the Courtyard,
where tall dahlias (not in flower) are underplanted with
mauve verbena, red pelargonium and crimson busy Lizzies.

FRONTISPIECE: Neat little terracotta pots filled with a range
of auriculas stand to attention in the Auricula Theatre at
Calke Abbey, Derbyshire for about six weeks, usually from
mid-April to the end of May.

Contents

Introduction

Whenever I stroll round National Trust gardens, it never ceases to amaze me how so few people can achieve so much. The exemplary standards of horticulture seen at most properties not only reflect the skill of the Head Gardeners and their staff, but also speaks volumes for their dedication. Gathered together, the vast knowledge and experience that the Trust's Head Gardeners possess would doubtless fill an encyclopedia: is it any wonder, then, that we lesser mortals, drawn to these gardens like bees to a honey-pot throughout the visiting season, continually stop them in their tracks in an attempt to prise as much horticultural information from them as possible?

Pots and Containers is the first in a new series of practical guides tackling specific gardening topics in response to this desire to tap into the Trust's deep reservoir of expertise. Fortunately the gardeners are a patient lot, very free with their tips and advice, and I am indebted to all who generously gave up their time to help me compile the information in this book.

It does not profess to tackle every aspect of container gardening, and sometimes may contradict the received wisdom of many textbooks. Indeed, you will find differences of opinion among the Head Gardeners themselves on such controversial issues as the control of pests and diseases. If anything, such conflicting views are healthy, proving that there is rarely one correct way to achieve a common end: this is how they do it and it works for them – but that is not to say it is the only way. Part of the satisfaction of gardening is having the opportunity to throw caution to the winds and experiment with unorthodox plants and methods: it is gratifying when the results are successful, but it is not the end of the world if they are not.

The gardens were chosen to give as broad a horticultural and geographical base as possible. The Tatton Park entry focuses primarily upon annuals for achieving summer colour in containers; Ickworth concentrates on perennials, while at Powis Castle the emphasis is on more tender plants. Sometimes there is a strong historical tradition for the use of pots and containers, as at Hanbury Hall, but often they are simply employed as a means of extending the season of interest, as is practised at Overbecks.

The final section of the book is devoted to the plants themselves. Of course the list is not exhaustive, but the great thing is to experiment – like the gardeners of the National Trust – and see what works for you in your own garden.

Cordyline, Bidens ferulifolia, Helichrysum petiolare and variegated ivy complement the stone urns of the Italian Garden at Tatton.

One of the pedimented niches in the brick wall in the centre of the Top Terrace at Powis Castle. In the time of the 2nd Marquess it would have been used to display sculptural busts, but now it provides a dramatic setting for a display of tender perennials. This is one of the combinations chosen by former Head Gardener Jimmy Hancock, with *Melianthus major* rising above *Fuchsia* 'Thalia' and *Tropaeolum* 'Hermine Grashoff'.

Powis Castle

The magnificent garden at Powis Castle is a plant lover's paradise. It boasts fine specimen trees and unusual shrubs in the woodland surrounding the castle, medieval stronghold of the Welsh princes. Powis is also home to an impressive collection of hardy and tender perennials on the four terraces that stretch out across the steeply sloping site below the building's imposing edifice. Container planting now plays an integral part in furnishing these Italianate terraces, thought to have been created for the 2nd Marquess of Powis between 1688 and 1722, and is also an important feature in the more formal Lower Garden.

Tintinhull

Tintinhull House Garden is relatively small compared with many National Trust properties. This does not mean the visitor is short-changed, though: far from it, for there is as much to learn from this delightful garden with its inspired use of plants and thoughtful design as there is from one twice the size. As is currently fashionable, the plot is divided into separate 'rooms' by tall, neatly clipped hedges and high walls, creating a number of smaller areas, each with its own distinct character. Pots and containers play an important role in the grand scheme of things, not only as design features in themselves, but also as a way of bringing quiet areas to life out of season.

The garden was created largely by Phyllis Reiss and her husband over a period of about 28 years, before being given to the National Trust in 1953. Although its concept and detail are entirely original, Mrs Reiss was greatly influenced by Hidcote (see pp. 11 and 32), a garden she used to visit regularly when she lived nearby. Her main intention at Tintinhull was to create year-round interest and beauty, an aim she expertly achieved. It is thanks to the work of the Trust and the sensitivity of successive tenants that the garden has retained so much of its original character and atmosphere more than a generation later.

Lilium regale Album Group in large pots placed against the west front of the eighteenth-century house at Tintinhull.

The famous Red Borders at Hidcote in May. Bronze cordylines stand ready to be plunged into the ground, where their spiky leaves provide a contrast to the salvias, dahlias and verbenas that give the borders their brilliant high summer colours.

Hidcote

Though they may never have paid homage to it, few gardeners have not heard of Hidcote Manor in Gloucestershire. Its reputation as one of the most important twentieth-century gardens is not to be underestimated, for its influence has spread far and wide, both in this country and abroad. Sissinghurst Castle and Tintinhull House are among the gardens within the National Trust that have drawn inspiration from it, and countless other private country house gardens including Newby Hall, North Yorkshire, and Barnsley House in Gloucestershire are indebted to Hidcote to some degree.

The 4-hectare (10-acre) site is largely divided into distinct areas to create a series of interconnecting spaces, or 'rooms', as they are commonly described nowadays. Each compartment, with its own atmosphere and theme, is surrounded mostly by tall evergreen hedges, needed as much for shelter on this exposed site high up in the Cotswold Hills as for their design potential. The crisp lines of hedges and paths, which make up the structural bones of the garden, are tempered by lavish planting schemes, in the main featuring loose, apparently self-sown drifts to create a natural effect.

Tatton Park

With its many surviving features, including an orangery, aviary, fernery, arboretum and maze, Tatton Park is a shining example of how gardens come to reflect the changing fashions of the age as well as the influences of their owners. Since 1715, until the death of Maurice in 1958, six generations of Egertons had been masters of Tatton, and all shared a passion for gardening. Famous horticulturists and designers, such as Humphry Repton, Lewis Wyatt and Sir Joseph Paxton, were all commissioned in their day, each one leaving an abiding mark on this 24.3-hectare (60-acre) garden. Today visitors can enjoy one of the most complete historic estates, which boasts not only a fine mansion, set within varied gardens and extensive parkland, but also a medieval great hall and a home farm, all little altered since they were bequeathed to the National Trust in 1958.

Calke Abbey

Not without reason is Calke Abbey known as 'the place that time forgot'. What the Trust found in 1985, when it accepted the house and garden from Henry Harpur Crewe, was a country estate surviving in its own bubble of tranquillity,

The auricula theatre in the Flower Garden, or Lady Crewe's Garden at Calke, one of three walled gardens now being restored to its former glory. It was installed by Georgina, Lady Crewe, in the early nineteenth century.

unaltered over the years, as if shut off from the modern world. Several members of the Harpur Crewe family were keen horticulturists. The Rev. Henry Harpur Crewe rescued from extinction a small yellow wallflower, *Erysimum cheiri* 'Harpur Crewe' and had other plants named after him. Georgina, Lady Crewe, chatelaine of Calke in the early nineteenth century, was a plant collector, notably of geraniums of which she had 58 varieties.

The mansion, erected on the site of a former Augustinian priory, was completed in the early years of the eighteenth century for Sir John Harpur. Between about 1770 and 1820 the original formal gardens, laid out by George London and Henry Wise, were replaced by the present pleasure grounds, characterised by undulating sweeps of grassland and strategically placed clumps of trees.

Hanbury Hall

In recent years Hanbury Hall, a relatively unknown 8-hectare (20-acre) property near Droitwich, has been the site of a major transformation. When Hanbury was bequeathed to the National Trust in 1953 by Sir George Vernon, in whose family it had always been, little of the garden existed around the William and Mary-style red brick house. That was to change in the autumn of 1993, when work began to reinstate the formal eighteenth-century layout of garden enclosures originally conceived by George London around 1700, but swept away when the formal style fell out of fashion.

Citrus aurantium var. *myrtifolia* 'Chinotto' in a wooden container outside the Orangery at Hanbury Hall.

The sword-like foliage of a variegated cordyline exploding like a fire-cracker amid *Fuchsia* 'Thalia' and *Pelargonium* 'The Boar', one of the tropical effects at Overbecks.

Overbecks

Overbecks is a gem of a garden. In the main, the National Trust endeavours and admirably succeeds in retaining the identity and character of each and every property it takes on, and this is particularly true of Overbecks. The moment you enter, you realise it is special. Admittedly, it does have several natural advantages, not least of which is its location, poised high on a precipitous hillside with unparalleled views across the shimmering Salcombe Estuary. This, together with its mild climate, abundant sunshine and free-draining, alkaline soil, make it favourable for the growth of a bewildering range of tender and subtropical plants. Bananas, cypress trees, olives, mimosas and Chusan palms all flourish outside, helping to create an atmosphere more usually associated with the Cote d'Azur than mainland Britain.

The garden was largely the creation of Otto Overbeck, who

bought the Edwardian property in the 1920s and bequeathed it to the Trust in 1937. A keen gardener, it was he who planted many of the *Trachycarpus* (Chusan palms). According to a local man, who was a garden boy in Overbeck's time, he was also keen on opuntias and agaves, which he bedded out to reinforce the fantasy.

Ickworth

There is something slightly surreal about Ickworth House near Bury St Edmunds. It is not just the vast scale that makes it appear larger than life: to chance upon such an intriguing piece of architecture with its immense Italianate rotunda in what appears to be an Italian setting in the middle of flat Suffolk countryside makes you feel you have somehow

One of the Victorian traditions continued at Ickworth is the display of blue African lilies. Overwintered in an unheated conservatory, these dramatic plants are brought out in the summer months to decorate the steps up to their winter home.

entered a time-warp and been transported to some other time and place.

Ickworth was the last and most grandiose of three building projects instigated by Frederick Hervey, 4th Earl of Bristol and Bishop of Derry in 1795. A self-confessed Italophile, he was passionately interested in travelling and collecting works of art, and the house, with its lofty central rotunda and two curving wings terminating in rectangular pavilions, was built more to display his pictures and sculptures than in which to enjoy mere domestic comfort.

Work on the house was not completed until 1829, 26 years after the Earl-Bishop's death, so it was his son and successor, Frederick, 1st Marquis of Bristol, who created the layout of the grounds. The design of the garden at Ickworth responds directly to the plan of the house: to the north, its long curving

In the West Courtyard at Belton, a former fountain head is a magnificent setting for the striking red *Pelargonium* 'Brunii' and the ivy-leaved *Pelargonium* 'L'Elégante'.

The herb garden with Bess of Hardwick's great mansion behind. At the time of writing, the wash coppers described on p.80 are submerged in scaffolding at the base of the South Tower.

arms embrace an oval lawn and sweeping flower border; to the south a matrix of gravel paths encloses lawns and a tapestry of predominately evergreen trees and shrubs, including evergreen oak, phillyrea, Italian cypress, holly and box, to give it a Mediterranean flavour. Some are used formally to line paths or edge green alleys, while others are planted informally in groups. It is interesting because it marks a return to a more formal style of gardening absent during the reign of Lancelot 'Capability' Brown and the English landscape movement, but it also predates the Victorian preoccupation with the Italian garden by several years.

Belton House

Constructed of local, honey-coloured limestone that seems to glow in the sunshine, the Restoration house of Belton in Lincolnshire makes a fine backdrop for the gardens that now surround it. Few traces survive of the original layout, which was elaborate and formal to complement the newly commissioned country house of 'Young' Sir John Brownlow in 1685. Like so many such schemes which fell prey to the tide of changing fashions, it was more or less swept away in the mid-eighteenth century by the new landscape style. The present formal layouts to the north of the house – the Italian Garden and the Dutch Garden – are largely the creation of the 1st and 3rd Earls Brownlow in the early and late nineteenth century respectively.

Hardwick Hall

Originally built for Bess of Hardwick, a veritable 'woman of substance' in her time, Hardwick Hall stands proud and defiant on top of a cold windswept escarpment. Although few alterations have been made to the imposing, square-topped edifice since it was completed in 1597, little remains of its Elizabethan garden, other than the surrounding walls, gazebos, finials and gateways.

What visitors enjoy today is chiefly the work of Lady Louisa Egerton, who laid out much of the south garden from the 1870s, with later additions by the National Trust, which accepted the property in 1959. Two bisecting grass alleys, bound by yew and hornbeam hedges, divide this 7-hectare (17.5-acre) square site into four major compartments. Orchards, lawns, nuttery and herb garden presently occupy these quadrants, and help to maintain the spirit of an Elizabethan garden in which even the redoubtable Bess of Hardwick would have felt comfortable.

Powis Castle

POWYS

Area: 10 ha (25 acres)
Soil: acid woodland, otherwise
 neutral to alkaline/clay
Altitude: 0–137m (0–450ft)
Average rainfall: 813mm (32in)
Average winter climate: cold

The man charged with the enviable, if not daunting, task of managing the garden grounds at Powis is Peter Hall, who is helped by a dedicated permanent staff of six, as well as occasional trainees and students. Peter took over as Head Gardener in the autumn of 1996, following the retirement of his predecessor, Jimmy Hancock, who was employed by the Trust for 25 years. Although there had always been a long tradition of inspired planting arrangements at the garden, Jimmy did much to put Powis Castle on the horticultural map by focusing attention on unusual tender perennials for use in the borders and in pots.

Undeniably, Jimmy is a tough act to follow, but Peter has already proved his mettle throughout his varied career working for the National Trust. He was first appointed Assistant Gardener at Wimpole, Cambridgeshire in 1978, followed by a spell as Gardener-in-Charge at Canons Ashby in Northamptonshire. He then spent ten years at Dunham Massey in Cheshire as Head Gardener, and eighteen months at Stourhead, Wiltshire, before succumbing to the lure of Powis and its wonderful range of plants.

Pots and containers at Powis

The use of plants in pots at Powis is not a new idea, although historically they would have been citrus trees, housed in the orangery throughout the winter months. It was the 4th Earl's wife, Violet, who really introduced flower gardening in the modern sense using pots and containers. Jimmy then developed the recent trend towards a mixed profusion of flowers and foliage, with the emphasis on experimenting with uncommon plants, a practice Peter hopes to continue. 'The containers have been excellent, so even though their contents may alter, I hope their concept will remain unchanged. Admittedly, they are quite labour-intensive in some respects, but if we can't do it at Powis, then who can? We've got the staff and the glasshouse facilities, which allow us the wonderful opportunity to propagate and grow on, so I hope very much that the tradition of container planting will continue.'

That said, Peter does feel there is a shortfall of colour throughout the garden early in the season, and is working on developing interest for this time of year. In the troughs he is considering more unusual spring bulbs such as fritillaries, scillas, anemones and dwarf narcissi. 'The problem is that if the garden is quiet, and you've got a container sitting there full of flowers, it could look as out of place as a very frothy hat in a supermarket!' he warns.

Powis boasts an impressive number of attractive terracotta pots, which are stored inside for the winter months, as well as several large stone troughs, lead urns and a copper container that are all permanently sited in the garden. Most of the terracotta pots are decorated with a basket-weave design, copied from the four originals used at Powis in Edwardian times. They are mainly used along the balustrades and at the end of flights of steps. There are also five tall, slim pots, which were specially commissioned about ten years ago to fit snugly into the five niches on the Top Terrace (see p.8).

Choosing a container

● To copy the effects achieved at Powis, remember big is beautiful, so go for the largest containers you can accommodate. When filled, they should provide ample compost and nutrients to sustain all the plants for an entire growing season, and should be heavy enough to prevent the whole display from blowing over in strong winds.

● The type of material used for the container is also important because it should complement its surroundings. At Powis terracotta works well with the orange-red brickwork predominant at the property.

Compost used at Powis

Plants in containers are rather like children: you can't expect them to do well in life unless you give them a good start and a nourishing diet. At Powis the compost is paramount to the success of the plants, from the nursery stage right through to the end of their time in potted displays. Kristian Booth, who has been Borders Supervisor there for six years, explains the system set up by Jimmy Hancock.

'We make all our own potting compost, which follows a basic John Innes formulation, but we also mix in slow-release fertiliser. We use our own loam, made up of composted, fibrous, coarsely chopped, sterilised turf. The coarseness of the compost depends on the stage of growth of the plant. For example, the loam will be sieved to make it finer for rooted cuttings, initially planted up in trays. A coarser grade will be used when potting them on, and by the time they go into their final containers, they will grow in the chunkiest grade of all. This coarseness is vital, as it makes for an open, free-draining medium, but being loam, it also retains moisture and nutrients. I would certainly recommend this method for containers, just from my own experiences of seeing the quality and results we have produced here.'

Making up the containers

● If your containers are too large to shift, make them up *in situ*, using plants that have been fully hardened off. At Powis all the terracotta pots are made up at the nursery from about mid-April in a large polythene lean-to. Here growth soon knits together and the plants are moved to their permanent summer quarters from mid-May, the tenderest subjects like *Fuchsia fulgens* braving the elements last of all. 'We always make sure the plants have obvious flower-buds when they go into the garden. This makes them less prone to being pilfered by the public for cuttings!' Kristian declares.

● Ensure adequate drainage by crocking the bottom of the pot. In the past at Powis broken terracotta crocks, shredded rubber tyres and Lytag (a waste product from power stations) have all been used for this purpose. They are presently trying out chunks of polystyrene, which they hope will make the pots lighter to lift.

● Half-fill the pot with compost, firm lightly and begin planting, placing the plant that grows tallest at the centre. At Powis the rest are positioned according to their eventual size and habit, finishing with trailing plants around the edge. Gently firm them all in, leaving a 5-cm (2-in) gap between the surface of the compost and the rim as a water reservoir and to prevent soil spillage. Water thoroughly.

● Stake tall plants with green split canes as a precaution against the wind or if you want to train plants into a shape. For the last three years the trailing stems of *Pelargonium* 'The Boar' have been tied in to provide height and a foliage back-cloth in the niches.

The way forward

Tender shrubs and perennials are the mainstays of the containers at Powis. Many flower continuously throughout summer; the majority have the kind of habit that works well in a potted display and, once hardened off, they tend to be more forgiving of frost than annuals. Being a keen propagator, Jimmy was responsible for introducing the rare and unusual species and cultivars associated with Powis. 'He always seemed to be one step ahead of the main nursery growers. At one time people just couldn't get hold of the plants we were growing. Some, like the double nasturtium, *Tropaeolum* 'Hermine Grashoff', are actually becoming more widely available because we used them,' says Kristian.

Peter hopes this trend will continue. 'I'm keen to try out pelargoniums, particularly the scented-leaved ones, as well as older species such as *P. blandfordianum*. It has soft, grey-green

Tropaeolum 'Hermine Grashoff'

Melianthus major (honey bush)

foliage and delicate, pinkish-white flowers, and should make a useful trailing plant for the edge of containers.' However, he also thinks there is a great deal of potential in using common plants in an unusual way. 'Plants don't have to be rare for me to consider them. I'm not a plant snob. I'll use anything if it works well,' he says.

Tried and tested favourites

The suggestions below have all passed the Powis test, and may inspire you to create your own versions. Flower colour, where applicable, is given in brackets. When planting up your containers, remember that shape and foliage are as important to the final effect as the flowers.

As a centrepiece
Salvia guaranitica 'Black and Blue' (dark blue)
Melianthus major (brownish-red)
Fuchsia 'Brutus' (red and purple)
Fuchsia 'Checkerboard' (white and red)
Fuchsia 'Coralle' (apricot-orange)
Fuchsia 'Gartenmeister Bonstedt' (brick-red)

As a trailer
Lotus berthelotii (orange-red)

As fillers and edgers
Bidens ferulifolia (yellow)
Diascia rigescens (pink)
Felicia amelloïdes (blue)
Helichrysum petiolare
Heliotropium 'Princess Marina' (deep violet-blue)
Pelargonium 'The Boar' (apricot)
Pelargonium 'Mrs Kingsbury' (pink)
Salvia discolor (indigo-black)
Tropaeolum 'Hermine Grashoff' (orange)
Verbena peruviana (scarlet)
Verbena 'Sissinghurst' (pinkish-red)

Fuchsias

Even the most unobservant visitor could not fail to spot that fuchsias, in all their guises, play an important part at Powis. Tall upright ones like the purple and scarlet 'Mission Bells' are favoured as centrepieces, while trailing ones such as the white and carmine 'Temptation' spill out over the edges of the containers. They flower for months on end, and some, notably those in the Triphylla group, which have long-tubed, single flowers, thrive in hot dry conditions. Although some are hardy, the majority in the garden are tender and need to spend the winter months under glass.

Those fuchsias used in the containers are grown very easily from cuttings taken the previous summer, with the exception of *Fuchsia* 'Machu Picchu'. Seldom without flowers, it is a

Fuchsia 'Coralle'

dream for the visitor, but a nightmare for the propagator because of its inconsiderate habit of producing flower at the expense of cutting material. It is therefore removed from the display at the end of the season, potted up and reused the following year, if necessary in one of the larger permanently sited containers. 'The thing with 'Machu Picchu' is that it can be upright and branching or low and spreading. You could possibly train it to do one thing or the other, but Jimmy always liked to make use of the plant's natural habit and not train it artificially,' explains Kristian.

Propagating fuchsias

At Powis cuttings are taken as soon as the non-flowering shoots appear, usually around August or September. Struck early, they normally make good root systems by the middle of October.

● Semi-ripe shoots, 8-10cm (3-4in) long, are cut from the parent plant, the lower half of the leaves removed flush with the stem, and the cutting trimmed just below a leaf node (**a**).

● The cuttings are then inserted around the edge of a shallow plastic pot containing cutting compost, made up of 50:50 peat (or peat substitute) and grit (**b**), and placed in a propagating frame. No heat is required at this time of year.

● Once well rooted, the cuttings are carefully removed and potted up into gravel trays, measuring about 60 × 30 × 8cm (24 × 12 × 3in), 24 plants to a tray (**c**). 'Not only does this save space in the greenhouses during winter, but Jimmy also felt the plants form better roots because they are not restricted,' says Kristian.

● When growth recommences, usually about mid-February, the cuttings are potted up into 10-cm (4-in) or 1-litre pots, depending on the size of their root-ball (**d**). 'If you want variety in the ultimate container, remember to use the smaller size of pot when potting up cuttings,' Peter advises.

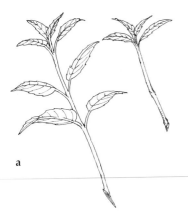

Propagating fuchsias, from taking cuttings to potting-up.

a

b

c

d

● By April the plants have filled their pots and are ready to be placed in the terracotta containers.

General propagation

There are two main propagation periods for cuttings at Powis:

● **August to mid-October.** Most of the container plants such as diascias, verbenas, and felicias will be propagated then, but towards the end of this period they are much slower to root because of decreasing temperature and light levels.

● **February to mid-March.** These cuttings are taken from over-wintered plants or from cuttings that were taken in autumn. Quick growers like helichrysum are propagated now to prevent them getting too large and swamping a carefully planned display.

A few plants such as bidens and *Oenothera cheiranthifolia* are grown from seed sown under glass in March. Although they could be vegetatively propagated, there is little point in overwintering cuttings and wasting valuable space in the greenhouse when they grow so easily from seed.

Summer maintenance

Watering is the major preoccupation with the containers. For the first month or so, they are watered about three times a week, but the pace is stepped up a gear come July, when they are checked daily. In the morning before the garden opens they are watered with a hosepipe, which is left in place until the water starts to drain through the bottom of the pot. To do all 21 pots on the terraces takes a minimum of one and a half hours, and the twelve or so in the lower garden take about half to three-quarters of an hour with a watering can. Extra feeding is not normally required because of the slow-release fertiliser already incorporated in the compost. Whenever possible, dead-heading and tweaking up is done at the same time as watering.

Tips

● When watering, drench the compost thoroughly, don't just splash water over the foliage. Stop as soon as it starts to run out of the drainage holes. If you overwater, too much fertiliser will be leached from the compost. Never rely on summer rainfall, as it only ever penetrates the top layer. The surface of the compost dries out quickest, so feeling the top will not indicate how dry the container really is. The best way to test the dryness of a terracotta pot is to tap its side: if it sounds hollow, water it.

● To prevent frost damage to fragile containers like those at Powis, empty them when the summer display is finished and store them in a shed for the winter. 'Ideally these types of containers should not be stacked inside each other,' says Peter, 'but if you cannot avoid it, then make sure they are packed with a good layer of straw between each one to stop them jamming tightly together.'

● Learn how to exploit natural microclimates by getting to know your garden, its hot spots and its shadier areas, and select plants accordingly. Not only will you be doing them a favour, you will be saving yourself a lot of time, money and wasted effort in the process. At Powis the high south-east facing walls of the terraces afford tender plants much shelter but they also act as a sun-trap in summer, with reflected heat bouncing off the stonework. Working with, and not fighting against, the natural conditions, by selecting the most appropriate plants in the first place, is the key to success in such circumstances. Salvias, lotus, felicias, pelargoniums and Mexican fuchsias can survive drought and revel in the baking hot conditions on the terraces, while *Diascia rigescens*, the blue pimpernel, *Anagallis* 'Blue Wonder', and the hardier fuchsias all fare better in the cooler Lower Garden.

● Don't be afraid to try out different plants in containers. Jimmy Hancock will probably be best remembered as the great experimenter. 'Even when he chanced upon a particularly good combination in the borders or containers, he would not necessarily use it a second year running. He always had new ideas and plants, acquired from his various trips away, that he wanted to try out,' remembers Kristian. Both she and Peter wholeheartedly agree with this notion. After all, that is what keeps the interest going. 'Planting in containers allows you to be adventurous, to try something new each year. Anyway, what may work one year, may be a failure the next because the weather is totally different. For me taking over at Powis, the repetition of success is not the primary concern; what is important is to carry on experimenting. That's healthy, I think. That's a good thing.'

Tintinhull House Garden

SOMERSET

Area: 0·8 ha (2 acres)
Soil: neutral/loam over
  marl clay
Altitude: 30 m (100 ft)
Average rainfall: 762 mm (30 in)
Average winter climate:
  moderate

Floyd Summerhayes is the man lucky enough to be Gardener-in-Charge at Tintinhull, although he is the first to admit that when he came for his interview as assistant to Penny Hobhouse, the former tenant of the property, he was less than enamoured by the place. 'It was a terrible, damp, foggy morning in March 1992,' he recalls, 'and the garden seemed very grey and dull. But I knew if I didn't take the opportunity, it could be years before a similar job came up in the Trust.' Fortunately any misgivings he may have had about leaving Nymans in Sussex, where he worked previously, soon melted away. 'Once you get involved in a place like Tintinhull it doesn't take long before you become totally absorbed by it.'

His promotion to Gardener-in-Charge came in 1992, when Penny and her husband left the property. He is helped by one other full-time gardener as well as a careership student. 'Just before Penny's departure we did a radio interview, which I hate hearing now. The first half was Penny; the next half was me talking about any changes I might make. At the time I can honestly say there were none planned, but then we had a bout of honey fungus and had to remove a number of large shrubs, which obviously altered the garden considerably. I think I must have been viewed as something of a hatchet man, even though the changes were forced on us,' he laughs. 'Now I think it is time to let the dust settle and allow our efforts to come to fruition.'

Pots and containers at Tintinhull

Although pots and containers were used at Tintinhull in the past, the displays were nowhere near as exuberant as they are today. 'It is the one element where we do not follow tradition here, which is largely a result of Penny Hobhouse's interest and expertise,' explains Floyd. 'I very much agree with her philosophy. It is the one time I can say to hell with it all, I don't have to follow convention. If I like a plant, I will give it a go, no matter what it is. I feel that even houseplants like chlorophytum have potential when used in containers.'

He is refreshingly enthusiastic about pots and containers, a subject obviously very close to his heart. 'The beauty of them is that if they don't work one year, it is a bit embarrassing, but you can change them easily enough the following season. Generally the public play too safe with them and grow the same old favourites all the time. My advice is to be a bit more adventurous. To me that is half the fun of it.'

His desire to experiment means that Floyd rarely keeps accessible records or takes photographs of his schemes, fearing he could get stuck into the rut of slavishly copying successful plantings every year. However, that is not to say he will alter the whole display simply out of principle: sometimes he may just change one plant. 'This garden is small, therefore you are much more likely to get bored with seeing the same plants every day. It is simply a way of encouraging renewed interest.'

Considerably more caution has to be shown in the Pool Garden. Not only are the four main stone tubs a prominent feature in themselves, but their contents also have to blend in with a pair of contrasting borders: one planted up with bold yellows, oranges and scarlet, the other with more muted pastel shades. In the past Floyd has experimented with a silver theme, using the feathery *Artemisia* 'Powis Castle', trained as a standard for the centrepiece, and *Lamium maculatum* 'White Nancy' together with *Lotus berthelotii* forming a skirt around the base of the pot. 'I like to play about with the shapes of the containers as much as anything,' he admits. 'Some years they are quite tall, others they are very rounded.'

Flexibility of container gardening

Pots and containers are used for a number of reasons at Tintinhull:

● as a strong design element in themselves, as with the four stone containers in the Pool Garden.

● to bring temporary colour to areas that would otherwise prove inhospitable for more permanent plants, for instance around the base of yew hedges.

● to accentuate the artificiality of gardening, as shown by the exotic white *Lilium regale* planted in large tubs on the west front of the house.

● as a means of adding colour to areas it would otherwise be impossible to cultivate, for example in the summerhouse.

● as a way of arranging a wide variety of individually potted specimens, brought out and displayed only when they are at their peak of flowering, and returned to more permanent quarters when they are past their best. Floyd is keen to make more of this technique, citing dianthus and lavenders, especially the tender *Lavandula pinnata*, and *Geranium maderense* as possible contenders.

Tulips in pots

For flower interest earlier in the year, about twelve containers are planted up with tulips. Two cultivars per pot (an early and

Tulips and forget-me-nots in small plastic pots being plunged into large stone containers.

a later flowering one) would have been used in previous years à la Hobhouse, but being Floyd, he decided to try something different. 'We had no end of complaints when we reduced the number of bulbs and added spring-flowering pansies as an underplanting instead,' he smiles. Recently forget-me-nots have also proved immensely valuable in extending the container displays. 'They are brilliant because they continue to flower long after the tulips have gone over. In fact they last right up to the end of May when we swap the spring bedding for the summer schemes.'

In the past tulips were planted up in containers as soon as they arrived, using the same compost that sustained the summer bedding, but recently Floyd has obtained very good results following a different method. This involves potting up the individual bulbs in early November into 9-cm (3.5-in) plastic pots, which are then plunged into a cold frame packed with bark chips. In March they are lifted and planted, pots and all, where they are to flower. Forget-me-nots, also grown on in pots, are slotted in around them in a similar manner, so creating a more or less instant display. 'Not only does this mean we can empty the stone containers and put protective covers on them for the winter, but it also allows us to remove at an early stage any tulips suffering from tulip fire, a fungal disease which distorts the foliage. As an added bonus, it is a quick and easy process to remove the entire display when it is over.'

Perennials in pots

In recent years pots and containers have been used to great effect within the summerhouse. Although south-facing, the two far recesses are quite shaded, causing the plants within the building to lean towards the light. Instead of slaving to grow Mediterranean plants such as olives that are traditionally associated with such a structure, Floyd decided to furnish the interior space with shade-loving species.

Lapping up the conditions there now and helping to create a luxuriant, tropical effect are rodgersias, hostas and the white arum lily, *Zantedeschia aethiopica* 'Crowborough'. 'My plan is to introduce variously sized plants, such as lamium and ferns, and build them up so that each one hides the pot of the one behind. This graded effect should give the impression that the plants are growing in a border and not in containers at all.'

Making up the containers

● Plant up your containers *in situ* when all risk of frost has passed: at Tintinhull this is done at the end of May.

● Remember that less is actually more when selecting your plants. 'For greater impact use two plants of three cultivars,

A small grouped display of plants for a shady spot. *Rodgersia*, variegated hosta, *Zantedeschia aethiopica* 'Crowborough' and *Lamium* 'White Nancy' are all shown here in their individual terracotta pots.

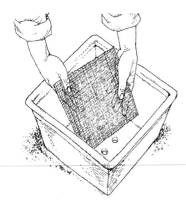

Placing zinc mesh over the drainage holes at the bottom of a container.

rather than six different varieties, particularly in smaller pots up to 35 cm (14 in) in diameter,' recommends Floyd.

● Place a piece of zinc mesh (the sort used in car body repairs) over the drainage holes of your chosen container. 'This stops compost clogging up the holes and prevents worms and wood lice burrowing up through it. I have found no further drainage material is required, allowing a greater volume of compost to be placed in the container, resulting in happier plants.'

● Fill the pot with compost to within about 2·5 cm (1 in) of the rim, and arrange the plants on the surface to get an impression of the final look.

● Starting in the middle and working out towards the edges, scoop out the compost and firm in your plants. Water in well using a rose on the watering can, cross your fingers and hope you do not get a late frost.

● When the plants have settled in, usually after about two weeks, give them a boost with a solution of seaweed fertiliser. No further feeding will be required if you have incorporated a slow-release fertiliser into the compost prior to planting.

Compost at Tintinhull

Floyd mixes his own compost which is used at every stage of growth from rooted cuttings right through to the main containers. This is made up by volume of:

2 parts sterilised loam or John Innes No. 3
1 part 0–5 mm Cornish grit
1 part peat, fine-grade bark or vermiculite
2·5 g slow-release fertiliser (Osmacote) per litre of compost
1 g water-retaining granules per litre of compost

He prefers a loam-based compost, not only because it is more moisture-retentive, but also because it promotes tighter, more resilient growth. 'Plants seem to grow too easily in a peat-based compost, producing long, lanky shoots,' he explains.

Planting suggestions

Although Floyd is always on the look-out for more plants to try, the following are some of his tried and tested favourites, together with some of his comments about them.

Anisodontea capensis Unusual salmon-pink flowers. Combine it with the similarly coloured *Diascia rigescens*.

Artemisia 'Powis Castle' Very useful in containers. Can be trained as a standard if clipped regularly.

Heliotropium 'Chatsworth' The best heliotrope with very sweetly scented, deep purple flowers.

Hibiscus trionum Useful annual with trumpet-shaped, creamy-yellow flowers each with a maroon centre.

Nemesia denticulata **'Confetti'** Valuable because it always seems to push its way up through other plants before producing its mauve flowers.

Salvia discolor Unusual blackish flowers and sticky glaucous foliage.

Pericallis lanata (**syn.** *Senecio heritieri*) Has striped blue and white, daisy-like flowers. Try it with the bicoloured pink and white *Verbena* 'Carousel' for a really striking combination.

Solenopsis axillaris (**syn.** *Isotoma axillaris*) We have been growing this under-rated plant for years. It produces mounds of starry blue flowers.

Verbena Very useful, long-flowering container plants. 'Silver Anne' has pink flowers that fade to whitish-pink; 'Imagination' has purple flowers and feathery foliage.

Lilies in pots

Historically Mrs Reiss grew regal lilies, *Lilium regale* Album Group, in large pots on the west front of the house, a tradition the National Trust has retained (see p.9). Not only do their white trumpets look stunning against the yellow Ham stone of the Queen Anne façade, but their intoxicating perfume also wafts on the breeze to scent still July evenings.

The lilies are replaced following a strict four-year rotation: the contents of each container are totally renewed once every four years to maintain a consistently impressive display. However, for the Trust's centenary year, it was decided to re-plant all four pots, despite the expense. That was all well and good, until the bulbs started to flower. 'They turned out to be multi-coloured, which didn't go down too well, as you can imagine,' remembers Floyd.

For lilies in pots he advises:

● Plant them as soon as they arrive to prevent the bulbs from drying out.

● Don't be mean. Cram in as many as you can, aiming to place them just one bulb's width apart, about 15-18cm (6-7in) deep in the pot (**a**).

● Allow the shoots to reach about 30cm (12in) before staking with a bamboo cane, taking care not to pierce the bulb in the process (**b**).

● Feed with half-strength liquid Phostrogen on alternate waterings. Dead-head the lilies to prevent seed formation, but allow the foliage to die back naturally. The stem should

Planting lilies in pots and staking the shoots.

a

b

require no more than a gentle tug once it is ready to come away from the bulb.

Plant propagation

Several years ago the National Trust invested in two pieces of equipment, known as 'Dewpoint Cabinets', which totally revolutionised propagation at Tintinhull. Inside each large, self-contained aluminium unit a thermostatically controlled heated tray warms a reservoir of water. Air is pumped through the water, creating a humid environment. When this warm, moist air touches the cool aluminium sides, it forms condensation which runs back into the reservoir.

The conditions the Dewpoint Cabinets produce are perfect for cuttings chiefly because moisture loss from the leaves is eliminated and rapid root growth is encouraged. Because the plants remain dry, common mould diseases are never a problem. 'It may just have been beginner's luck, but the first year we had them, all but one of the 3,500 cuttings we took rooted,' declares Floyd. 'They are brilliant, but their main drawback is the expense: each unit costs about £370. Also we have never found them very satisfactory for seeds, which just grow too tall and leggy, almost before our very eyes.'

Owing to the lack of greenhouse space, only stock plants are overwintered. The main thrust of the bulking up is done in February when the parent plants are stripped of cuttings. If further plants are required later on, the nipped-out shoots of these cuttings will be rooted. 'One year we tried doing it all from cuttings taken in September, but we simply ran out of space because the plants grew too large.'

Usually the cuttings measure about 8–10cm (3–4in) long, and are inserted into a pot or tray containing pumice gravel, before being placed in one of the Dewpoint Cabinets. 'The advantage of this medium is that it is volcanic in origin, so we can sterilise it under high temperatures and then reuse it,' Floyd explains.

Most of the tender perennials will be propagated in this way; so too will some of the annuals raised from seed the previous year. 'Before we get too busy in spring I usually pay a visit to all the local garden centres just to have a nose through their seed section. If something new or different catches my eye, I bring it back, sow it, and if I like it I will propagate it from cuttings in subsequent years, using only material from the colours or forms I find attractive. This is not only cost-effective, but it also means we get the shades we like. And since seed germination can be erratic, taking cuttings guarantees we have the quantities we need early in the season.'

Natural plant supports

One of Floyd's aims at Tintinhull is to reintroduce traditional methods of horticulture wherever possible. 'It worries me a bit that no one is saving the techniques of gardening because they are all so busy saving the plants. Admittedly this would probably generate more work for us, but because the garden is small, I feel we could cope with the labour it would entail.'

As an example, he pinpoints using willow as a means of supporting plants, particularly those in containers. Instead of tying the lilies to individual canes, he wants to bend over long lengths of willow to produce a kind of cage. 'Not only is it a locally grown product, but it could also be an attractive and unusual feature in itself,' he explains. 'Its main problem is that it roots too easily. To use it in the garden you have to kill it first, but somehow retain its flexibility. With this in mind, we have just invested in a tea urn so that we can bundle up the stems and boil both ends. We are hoping this will do the trick.'

Tips

Using circular ring stakes as plant supports in a potted display.

● If you are nervous about trying different colour combinations in containers, experiment first with a large plastic pot that is tucked away unobtrusively in a corner. Floyd has an area of the nursery where he can experiment with any surplus stock. Remember to note down any comments or changes you want to make to the scheme for the following season.

● Use circular ring stakes instead of tying fragile or vulnerable growth to individual canes in a windy or exposed spot. More commonly promoted for herbaceous plants, they are just as good in containers, particularly if you choose one with the same diameter as your pot. Position the support early so that the plants will grow up through and eventually hide it.

● If you cannot afford decorative containers or will have no truck with plastic ones, why not paint large terracotta pots a colour that will complement their surroundings? Phyllis Reiss painted hers with emulsion until she found a shade that suited the yellow Ham stone of her house.

● Use a sharp pair of scissors rather than secateurs for deadheading. They make it much easier to get in among the stems, even when working with roses.

● Don't be too quick to blame yourself if a plant does not flourish. 'Gardeners generally assume they are responsible, but sometimes the fault lies with the plant. Here at Tintinhull we give a plant three chances. If it does not thrive after that, we abandon the idea of using it,' says Floyd.

Hidcote Manor Garden

GLOUCESTERSHIRE

Area: 4 ha (10 acres)
Soil: alkaline
Altitude: 183 m (600 ft)
Average rainfall: 635 mm (25 in)
Average winter climate: cold–
   very cold

In charge of the high-profile garden at Hidcote Manor is Paul Nicholls, a straight-talking, down-to-earth type, who professes to prefer the term 'gardening' to 'horticulture', because it sounds more friendly. A good all-rounder, he gained experience in commercial as well as amenity horticulture and worked at the Botanic Gardens in Edgbaston, Birmingham before settling at Hidcote in 1972. Six years later he was made Head Gardener.

Surprisingly for such a significant garden, few records remain. Its creator, Lawrence Johnston, did not keep any notes or garden diaries, and there is little evidence of any master plan. It simply evolved over 40 years, as his interest in gardening and plants grew. In 1948 the National Trust took the unprecedented step of accepting Hidcote from Johnston on account of its garden, the owner having made up his mind to live out the rest of his days on the French Riviera.

Pots and containers at Hidcote

When Lawrence Johnston died in 1958, much of his personal estate was sold. A number of pots and containers found their way into the sale and were duly dispersed; therefore it is reasonable to assume that many more were used in Johnston's day than are employed here now. 'Trying to find out where they have gone is like looking for the proverbial needle in a haystack,' says Paul.

Today, most of the containers at Hidcote are planted up to extend interest and colour throughout summer and into autumn. 'Because we are open to the public, our main criterion has to be to provide flower colour for the visitors. Those with no one else to please but themselves can plant up their containers for different reasons,' he says. In Lawrence Johnston's case a plant had to offer more than just colour to find a place in his heart. Its overall shape, habit of growth and foliage were of equal importance.

Entry to the garden is via the Garden Yard, just beyond the ticket office. Here four large, square, wooden tubs, known as Versailles cases, spill over with fuchsias, to create a positive first impression. To heighten the impact just two cultivars, both of which occurred naturally at Hidcote, are used in alternating containers. 'Hidcote Pink' has upswept, creamy white sepals, often faintly tinged green, and a pale pink skirt, while 'Hidcote Hybrid' is very similar but has a much deeper pink bell. Interestingly, the two growing against a north-facing wall flower just as well as the ones that receive more light.

A little further along in front of the garden workshops, two square wooden citrus boxes are planted with a vivid red zonal pelargonium which makes a striking foil to the blue painted woodwork of the stores behind. Yellowish-green *Helichrysum petiolare* 'Limelight' provides the display with bulk and balance. To this Paul likes to add a dash of purple-bronze foliage for contrast, either in the form of perilla, if he can obtain the seed, or basil 'Purple Ruffles'.

A long, narrow lead cistern completes the container planting in the Garden Yard. Here the vanilla-scented, mid-blue *Heliotropium* 'Lord Roberts' holds sway, along with the grey-leaved *Helichrysum petiolare*. Surprising though it may sound, both appear to be thriving in this shaded position.

This marriage of blue and grey is also a popular choice for the Old Garden. Two large Italianate terracotta pots, now apparently settled on either side of its entrance gate, feature both heliotrope and helichrysum, as well as the impossible sounding *Centaurea cineraria* ssp. *cineraria* (syn. *Centaurea gymnocarpa*), or dusty miller, as it is more appealingly known. Lifted and coaxed on in the glasshouse during winter, it makes an unusual but attractive centrepiece with its silver, ferny foliage. The tender perennial *Lobelia richardsonii*, with its trailing habit and light blue flowers, adds frothiness to the display.

Similar colours are also to be used in the five Versailles cases that line the side path in the Old Garden. Until recently these contained permanent plantings of white *Hydrangea arborescens* 'Grandiflora', but over the years their vigour had declined to such an extent that Paul decided to replace them with summer bedding. 'I think a very luxuriant planting scheme would suit the location,' he says. Therefore his current plans are to fill them with more dusty miller, *Argyranthemum* 'Sark', which is a small, double, white marguerite, and *Osteospermum* 'Blue Streak', whose slate-blue central boss provides a vivid contrast to its shining white petals. He hopes the semi-climbing blue *Clematis* × *durandii* will scramble up from the border behind and mingle with the display. 'At Hidcote we can be fairly autonomous with the summer bedding because we know the sort of plants that are sympathetic to Lawrence Johnston's aims. However, because we only have two small glasshouses and a plastic tunnel, we are limited to what we can raise by these facilities.'

Perennials in pots

As well as the temporary summer bedding displays, the garden at Hidcote boasts a number of plants that are permanently settled in containers:

Hosta sieboldiana The huge, glaucous blue foliage of this hosta makes a handsome sight in its large terracotta pot in the courtyard outside the Italian summerhouse. As far as Paul can recollect, it has never been divided or repotted; therefore its lush, healthy appearance must be down to the rejuvenating top-dressing of well-rotted manure it receives each spring.

Rhus glabra '**Laciniata**' A matching pair of potted sumachs grow alongside the hosta. With its deeply toothed pinnate foliage, which turns brilliant orange-scarlet in autumn, *Rhus glabra* 'Laciniata' makes a most elegant shrub or small tree. To encourage larger leaves, as well as to maintain a balance between the top growth and container, the new growth is pruned back in early spring to within a few centimeters (1 in) of the old wood. Top-dressing with John Innes No. 2, together with occasional liquid feeds throughout summer, keeps the shrubs healthy.

Agave americana '**Variegata**' Stiff and architectural with piercingly sharp foliage, several agaves adorn the lily pool in the Pine Garden as well as the brick paving in Mrs Winthrop's Garden. As tough as old boots, they receive little more than the occasional watering and feeding after they are placed in position in late May or early June. However, come October they are taken under cover where they spend the winter months in a plastic tunnel, heated just enough to keep it above freezing. When the plants start to look untidy, the gardeners don stout leather gauntlets and repot them using a standard John Innes No. 2 mix to which extra grit is added for improved drainage. At this point any offsets which have formed at the base of the agave are pulled away or removed with a sharp knife and potted up.

Cordylines With their great sword-like bronze sheaves, no one could accuse the cordylines at Hidcote of slipping quietly into the background. Their architectural form lends a particularly tropical feel to Mrs Winthrop's Garden, where three specimens, about 0·9–1·2m (3–4ft) tall, are placed on raised brick platforms for the summer months. A further eighteen or so also provide dramatic contrast in the twin red borders, where they are planted among exotic cannas, vibrant dahlias and lush day-lilies, to name but a few (see p.11).

To speed up the bedding-out process, they are simply plunged into the soil in their pots in May. When they are lifted from the borders in November to be returned to the heated plastic tunnel, each planting hole is not filled in but is replaced by an empty plastic pot with the same dimensions. A small cane marking its position is the only indication of its existence

Propagating cordylines, removing the 'toes' with a sharp knife.

after a mulch of well-rotted manure has been applied to the entire border in autumn. Come May, the empty pots are removed and once again replaced by the cordylines, and so the cycle continues.

Cordylines are propagated between January and February. They are knocked out of their pots, the compost is shaken off and the small knobbly growths, or 'toes', are removed with a sharp knife. Paul sometimes uses a saw if the parent plant is old and is to be discarded anyway. The toes are then potted into 9-cm (3.5-in) pots containing cutting compost, and placed on a heated propagating bench to root.

Cultivation of fuchsias

As the fuchsias 'Hidcote Pink' and 'Hidcote Hybrid' are now considered to be so much part of the fixtures and fittings at the property, Paul is anxious not to lose them. To prevent them looking out of scale in their wooden cases in the Garden Yard, they have to be installed as large plants. Paul used to lift the old plants and reuse them, but he now finds they make more luxuriant growth and flower more prolifically if he renews them from cuttings every year. To obtain decent-sized plants he offers the following advice:

● Take cuttings in August for the following season. Softwood cuttings from fast-growing stem tips, about 6–8cm (2.5–3in), should root within about three weeks.

● Once rooted, transfer the cuttings to 9-cm (3.5-in) pots and grow on in the greenhouse. Periodically pot them up into larger containers once the roots are visible on the outside of the soil ball. The fuchsias at Hidcote often come out of 25-cm (10-in) plastic pots by the time they are planted out the following June.

● To obtain shapely plants that are well-clothed with branches, pinch out the growing tip when the young plant is about 15cm (6in) tall. This will encourage the formation of side shoots, which can also be nipped back if they become too long. The more you 'stop' them, the bushier the resulting plant will be. Paul prefers his plants to have a loose lax habit, therefore he will not be over zealous with this pinching back.

Nipping back or 'stopping' fuchsias to encourage branching.

General propagation

At Hidcote most of the plants are propagated from cuttings. Timing is the most important criterion for success, according to Paul. Most plants, like heliotropes, will root in no time if taken from August to late September from semi-ripe cuttings. A propagating unit, incorporating heated cables below and mist overhead, like the one used at Hidcote, will encourage

Sprinkling silver sand over the surface of potting compost to improve drainage for cuttings.

speedy rooting, but a simple plastic propagator or even a polythene bag placed over the pot of cuttings will be just as good, especially if small numbers of plants are required.

Grey-leaved plants, such as dusty miller and helichrysum, are best propagated in late winter or early spring from 8-cm (3-in) long cuttings. Because silver-leaved plants are much more susceptible to rot, they should be placed on the very edge of the mist unit. If they become dry, a light misting from a hand sprayer is usually all that is needed to keep them moist, but never wet.

'A useful tip when taking all cuttings is to spread a layer of silver sand over the top of the compost, so that when you insert a dibber some of the sand will fall into the hole and help improve drainage round the bottom of the cutting,' explains Paul.

Planting up the containers

Situated 183 m (600ft) up in the north Cotswold Hills, Hidcote is prone to late spring frosts. 'I don't believe in dicing with death,' Paul says firmly, 'so I wait until June before setting out the bedding. Unfortunately this means that most of the plants will be covered in flowers and may get a bit of a check in growth. They may sulk for a while, but they soon perk up.'

Paul fills the containers with as many plants as he can. Because they have already produced a good deal of growth, he always ensures he turns them first before planting them with their best sides outermost.

Compost and fertilisers

There is nothing arcane about the compost used in the containers at Hidcote. 'We simply use a good quality bought-in compost to which we add well-rotted manure for its moisture-holding qualities.' Both fast- (Vitax Q4) and slow-release (Osmacote) fertilisers are also incorporated. The first gives the plants the early kick-start they require, while the second is activated when soil temperatures exceed 21°C (70°F).

As a rule the entire compost in the large, permanently sited containers is only replaced every four or five years when the quality of the plants begins to decline. Otherwise they are simply backfilled with fresh compost when the old bedding is removed. However, the two Italianate terracotta pots, which are emptied and brought in every winter for protection, are treated to new soil each season.

Spraying programme

Whitefly and aphids are the main pest problems in the glasshouses and occasionally outside in the gardens at Hidcote.

Paul is the first to admit that he doesn't mind using chemicals to eradicate them. 'Admittedly it is not a pleasant job, and nobody really enjoys doing it, but I do not understand the logic of people with an aversion to using chemicals. If you're ill you go to a doctor, if your pet is sick you take it to a vet, so if your plants are not in good health, don't you treat them?' he asks provocatively.

Unfortunately whitefly in particular are now beginning to build up resistance to many insecticides. This is compounded by the fact that the range of products available for use is decreasing year upon year as some are no longer approved for use and are subsequently withdrawn from the market. 'We have found that using a rotation of two or three different chemicals in our spray programme limits this problem of resistance,' he says. Of those still available to the amateur grower, Paul recommends alternating a combination of products, for example Py Garden Insecticide, Rapid and Murphy Tumblebug each time you spray.

Despite his preference for chemical controls, he finds that damping down the greenhouses during hot spells, beginning as early as March, keeps many of the worst offenders at bay.

Tips

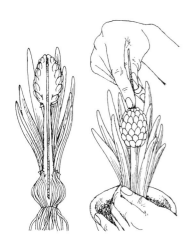

Inserting a stout piece of wire through a hyacinth stem and bulb.

● As an insurance policy against losing your prized tender perennials during the winter, ensure you lift at least one of each variety to use as a stock plant before the frosts set in. Pot them up, and grow them on in a greenhouse or frost-free place. Propagate them as soon as the material is available, and only discard the stock plant when you know your cuttings have rooted.

● If you find hyacinth flowers loll about drunkenly in their containers, try treating them as the Dutch do. It may sound brutal, but poking a stout wire through the flowering stem right down to the core of the bulb will ensure that they stand as upright as sentry guards. The bulbs should not be used again to avoid spreading infection.

● Success with containers is almost assured if you get the basics right in the first place. Not only does this mean using a good quality compost, but you should also start with healthy plants. You must be prepared to look after them, watering and feeding them as necessary, dead-heading them frequently to encourage more flowers, and always keeping a look-out for pests and diseases and treating them accordingly.

Tatton Park

CHESHIRE

Area: 24·3 ha (60 acres)
Soil: acid / sand
Altitude: 60 m (197 ft)
Average rainfall: 711 mm (28 in)
Average winter climate: cold

The man charged with overseeing the gardens at Tatton Park is energetic Liverpudlian Sam Youd, whose indomitable spirit allows him to rise to and overcome any challenge put to him. Most of us might imagine that being responsible for the smooth running of such gardens would be more than enough for anyone to cope with, but Sam reels off all his other sidelines – lecturer, writer, regular guest on radio and television, not to mention joke teller! By his own admission, he is involved with 'anything and everything to do with gardening.'

Sam came to Tatton in 1979 as propagator, following a long and varied career at Liverpool Parks Department. 'My final job there was as technical adviser, but going to work in a suit and sitting in an office with a secretary, six filing cabinets and four telephones was not my idea of fun. So I packed it all in and came here, originally with the intention of staying just three years, but that was seventeen years ago!' In 1983 he became Head Gardener and has never looked back. 'Tatton is such a great place to work, not only because of the range of plants, but because there is such potential and scope. Since coming here, we have restored the Italian Garden, Orangery, Fernery and Show House. The Japanese Garden is next, and the restoration of the Kitchen Garden is on the cards for 1998.' With all this going on, Sam makes full use of his staff of fourteen gardeners.

Pots and containers at Tatton

Although Tatton is steeped in history, container planting does not necessarily follow any time-honoured tradition. The two main reasons for employing it are to extend the period of interest and as a strong design element.

In 1856, Sir Joseph Paxton supplied plans for the formal Italian-style garden stretching out below the porticoed south front of the mansion, but work on it did not actually begin until 1890. It was around this time that the Italian marble vases were moved from the Orangery to the top of the retaining wall overlooking the parterres – a position they still enjoy today (see p.6).

Planting within the vases and parterres tends to be rather muted to avoid detracting from the magnificent views of the mere and surrounding parkland. Pinks, blues, white and silver dominate the summer schemes and work in well with the greyish colour of the marble, which itself can look somewhat drab. Cordylines as centrepieces, frothy blue trailing lobelia, helichrysum and a light peppering of yellow *Bidens ferulifolia* for impact are the main ingredients of the vase displays. In winter the vases are emptied out and covered to provide protection from frost and pollution.

Small and intimate, the Rose Garden was laid out around 1913 with a sunken patio, formal pool, garden shelter and flanking pergola. It is a bright, light, airy place, and plans are afoot to introduce four large terracotta pots filled with blue and white agapanthus to complement the existing planting.

In total contrast to the Rose Garden, the adjoining Tower Garden, with its red brick, battlemented, square folly, is overshadowed by high walls and a large yew tree. A lead urn and lead tank at the base of the tower are planted up to reflect the subdued, rather gloomy atmosphere of the enclosure, using 'Tom Thumb' fuchsias for summer, and rosemary and low-growing sedum for winter.

One of the first impressions visitors have of Tatton is of the Stable Yard. It is an important focal point because it is a main car park and the garden entrance, shop and refreshment area are situated there. The estate is open all year round, so it is vital that the Stable Yard looks appealing even in the depths of winter. This is no mean feat, given the expanse of soulless tarmac, heaven for well-heeled visitors, but hell for Sam who has to soften the effect with plants to make it look less stark.

A generous number of strategically sited, wooden half-barrels are part of his quick-fix solution, together with mangers, used as hanging baskets, fixed to the brick walls of the surrounding buildings. He likes his planting schemes to have impact, to act as an enticement, so he opts for bright, multi-coloured flowers, which he laughingly refers to as 'a chorus girl's washing line' – a term coined by a previous employer. This goes a long way in achieving the 'ooh and aah' factor he feels is so important.

Plants for mangers and hanging baskets

The mangers are sited on two separate buildings. Plants that enjoy the sunny, south-facing aspect are numerous. Some of the most dependable and free-flowering are *Begonia* 'Non-stop', pelargoniums, *Bidens ferulifolia*, petunias and verbenas. The selection for the opposite, north-facing wall is much less extensive, but good stand-bys include fuchsias, lobelias, *Brachycome iberidifolia* and *Helichrysum petiolatum*.

The summer displays in the half-barrels tend to mirror the plants in the mangers above them so that an element of continuity is maintained. The main difference will be the inclusion of a centrepiece to give height to the middle of the container. Variegated abutilons, grevilleas, hedychiums, standard fuchsias and *Eucalyptus globulus*, with its rounded, juvenile, blue-grey foliage, are all top contenders for this central position.

Groups of three half-barrels have also been used to break up the large expanse of tarmac. Here just one variety will be used for the greatest impact. *Verbena rigida* (syn. *V. venosa*), heliotrope, bidens, the dependable double red *Pelargonium* 'Caroline Schmidt' with variegated green and white foliage, and the scented-leaved, white-margined *P.* 'Lady Plymouth' have all been used successfully in the past.

There are also a number of permanently planted half-barrels containing individual specimens of box, cordyline or the spreading, glossy evergreen *Prunus laurocerasus* 'Otto Luykens'. Sam has devised an ingenious method whereby the main plant is actually potted into a large, plastic tree container with sturdy handles before being plunged into the half-barrel. This enables compost and annuals to be replaced easily around the margin of the barrel when necessary.

Spring bedding at Tatton

This is an important aspect for all the wooden barrels in the Stable Yard because the garden is open throughout the year. What Sam decides to use depends on which plants are surplus to requirements in the bedding schemes around the estate.

The containers here are normally planted up in October, as soon as the summer display begins to look jaded. Forget-me-nots are among Sam's favourites for underplanting. They do best in a partially shaded spot in moist soil; if they dry out, they often succumb to mildew. He also recommends wall-flowers for pots, especially in gardens where they are usually ravaged by rabbits if planted on terra firma. Single colours, such as the crimson *Erysimum cheiri* 'Blood Red', which will flower at the same time make more impact than a mixed batch.

Polyanthus are good too. 'We collect and save our own seed in about July because we have an old variety at Tatton that we want to keep. The plants cross-pollinate so we have now got a really good mix of pure, clear colours, which are so much nicer than modern bicolours,' he explains. To maintain their vigour, fresh stock is sown every year; the plants are never retained. Polyanthus are biennials, so they must be sown one season to flower the next. Sam's timetable is as follows:

● Sow the seed under glass in October, and prick out into seed trays when the first true leaves have formed.

● Carefully remove the young plants from the seed trays and in April line them out in a nursery bed outside to allow them to grow on. Water in dry weather.

● Move the plants to their ultimate flowering positions in October, spacing them about 23 cm (9 in) apart.

● Clear the plants away after they have flowered, discarding all but the best ones, which will be retained for seed. Heel in these selected polyanthus in an unused corner of the garden and collect the seed when ripe, usually around June.

Bulbs, usually tulips, are then placed in and around the underplanting. For a reliable display:

● Select good quality bulbs that are plump and free of disease and physical damage.

● Plant the bulbs in November, about 13 cm (5 in) deep, 8 cm (3 in) apart.

● Unless the site is sheltered from wind, avoid tulips with tall stems, elegant though they may be. Sam recommends 'Flair', which is reddish-orange and 20 cm (8 in) tall, and 'Keizerskroon', which has scarlet flowers edged with yellow and grows to about 30 cm (12 in). The Kaufmanniana and Greigii types are ideal for containers as they are short, come in a wide colour range and are often blessed with attractive mottled foliage; the former flowers in March, the latter in April.

Winter displays for mangers and hanging baskets

Winter hanging baskets are notorious for being either dull or just plain unreliable, because the weather can be so capricious. Sam has devised an ingenious way round the problem. He cuts lengths of evergreen foliage, such as variegated holly, ivy and conifers, and pokes them through the sides of the basket (**a**). Pack in enough material and the display will hold itself firm and last all winter. Any odd shoots that become unsightly or shrivel up can be replaced easily.

The well in the middle of the basket can be used to hold seasonal plants, still in their pots, and swapped over as necessary (**b**). Berberis, mahonia, golden conifers or attractive

Creating a winter display for a hanging basket using evergreens and plants with autumn berries.

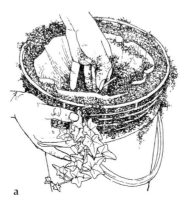

a   b

forms of holly are all suitable. Cones, together with autumn berries and hips, could also be inserted, and maybe even sprayed silver or gold for a truly festive look. For special occasions, arrange a bunch of flowers in a milk bottle or jar filled with water, and tuck that into the middle of the display.

Propagation

Vast numbers of plants are required for the displays at Tatton. Fortunately Sam can depend on a crew of willing propagators and nursery staff to supply him with all the plants he needs. Other than the standard fuchsias, all the plants for containers are grown afresh each year from cuttings or seed.

Cuttings

Cuttings of early flowering species such as the yellow daisy-like *Euryops acraeus* and perennial wallflowers are taken from June to July, and inserted straight into the prepared soil (50:50 peat and sand) of a cold frame. They root readily at this time of year, and are potted up in September or October to spend the winter months in an unheated plastic tunnel.

Cuttings, such as penstemon, helichrysum and fuchsia, which are taken later in the season from September to October, root best with bottom heat and overhead mist, both of which are provided by a propagating unit.

Seed

Much of the summer colour in the containers will come from half-hardy annuals, such as petunia, verbena and lobelia. Sam's nursery staff start sowing the seed at weekly intervals as soon as it arrives, usually in February. The first to be sown are species such as grevillea and pelargonium which require a long growing season, and last are rapid growers like nicotiana. With literally thousands of seedlings germinating at a constant rate, pricking out is a mammoth task and requires much greenhouse and frame space. Depending on what it is and where it is to be used, each seedling will be potted on at least once, sometimes twice, before reaching its final destination.

Compost

Except for sowing seeds and rooting cuttings, a soil-based compost (one that contains loam) is favoured for every stage of the plant's life at Tatton. 'We are great believers in loam-based compost here. If the plants are not introduced to it early enough, you get into all sorts of problems with watering – either they dry out too quickly or they stay too wet. They undoubtedly make good root systems in soil-less composts when they have just germinated, but then they have to make it in the real world. The sooner that the plants get used to growing in loam – which is a richer source of nutrients anyway – the healthier they will remain, particularly if they are destined for the containers, which can be a fairly hostile environment.'

At Tatton, they make their own potting compost, based on a typical John Innes No. 3 formulation, which by volume is:

7 parts sterilised loam
3 parts peat (or peat substitute)
2 parts sand
John Innes potting base (see below)

Although John Innes potting base is readily available, Sam prefers to make his own.

To each cubic metre of compost is added and thoroughly mixed:	The equivalent imperial conversion for one cubic yard of compost is:
594g ground limestone or 1·2kg hoof and horn	1lb ground limestone or 2lb hoof and horn
1·2kg superphosphate of lime	2lb superphosphate of lime
594g potassium sulphate	1lb potassium sulphate

'We make our own loam at Tatton because there is no substitute for all the fibre it contains,' explains Sam. They follow the time-honoured tradition of removing turves from the parkland and stacking them upside-down to form a hollow rectangle. The space inside the four turf walls is filled with general garden waste and soil. The heap is built up systematically with three layers of turf followed by one of leaf-mould and a generous scattering of lime. Composting is complete after about two years.

Planting up mangers and hanging baskets

At Tatton the mangers are fixed 5–8cm (2–3in) away from the walls to prevent water running down and causing problems to the building. To retain the compost, a piece of plastic board is cut to fit and fixed to the back of the manger, while a mould of chicken wire is used to line the sides. To all intents and purposes, it is now treated as a conventional hanging basket, except that it must be planted up *in situ*. Sam offers the following advice for both types of container:

● Before you start, sit the hanging basket on a bucket or large pot to keep it stable and clear of the ground or bench.

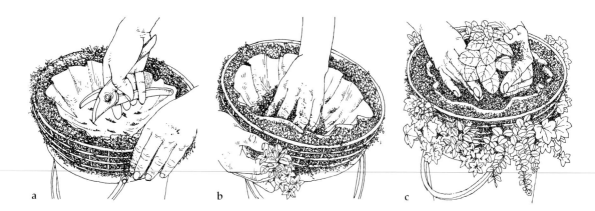

a   b   c

Planting up a hanging basket over a bucket to keep it clear of the ground.

● Line the inside of the basket with a layer of tightly packed, moist, live sphagnum moss. To help retain water, follow this with a lining of black polythene, through which you puncture a few holes for drainage (**a**).

● To camouflage the bottom and sides, carefully insert the trailing plants, making a hole in the polythene and guiding their root-balls through from the outside (**b**). Firm in well to stop them from being washed out when you water.

● Build up the display, adding more trailing plants and compost as you go.

● Continue until the compost is about 2·5cm (1in) from the rim, then plant more upright specimens in the centre (**c**).

● Water in well.

Wooden half-barrels

One of the subjects about which Sam can wax lyrical is the use of wooden half-barrels. At Tatton they presently contain exuberant bedding displays, but he has also earmarked them for use as water features in the conservatories where they will hold aquatic plants and water lilies. However you utilise them, remember Sam's advice:

● Buy barrels from a known source, and avoid any that were used to hold detergents or noxious chemicals. Beer, wine and cider barrels are among the best. The shallow type used at Tatton are known as puncheon barrels.

● Ensure that you fix the metal bands in place to prevent the individual laths splaying out when they dry and shrink. Do this by drilling a hole and screwing every fourth or fifth one. If you order them directly from the supplier, he will probably enquire if you want them to be cut, the bands fixed and the barrel varnished – answer yes to all three questions.

● Unless you want them as a water feature, drill about five 2·5-cm (1-in) holes at the bottom for drainage.

• To increase its life, preserve the inside of the barrel by charring it with a blowlamp.

• If you have to store an empty barrel, cover it with a sheet of polythene or sacking to maintain the humidity and prevent shrinkage. If the individual laths become loose, immerse the whole thing in water for a couple of days to swell the wood.

Planting up wooden half-barrels

As the Stable Yard retains heat reflected by the buildings, planting up the summer displays can be carried out as early as the beginning of May. In less favoured spots delay the operation until all risk of frost has passed.

• Begin by placing a generous layer of bricks on the bottom of the barrel for drainage.

• Cover the bricks with a layer of chopped turf, green side down, and spread with well-rotted farmyard manure.

• Fill to within 2.5–5cm (1–2in) of the top with loam-based compost and plant as necessary.

'As soon as their roots hit the manure the plants really go for it. If the compost dries out a little the roots are forced to go down in search of moisture, thereby encouraging a well-branched root system that ensures the plant is well-anchored. Thereafter they are better able to tolerate baking hot conditions and occasional drought,' explains Sam.

Food and water

Depending where they are, the containers can be watered up to twice a day at the height of summer. The mangers on the shady north wall, for example, will require less water than those facing south. Timing is important to avoid scorching the foliage and unnecessary evaporation. 'We tend to water outside visiting hours, either early in the morning or late at night, using a hosepipe with a lance attachment.' Water-retaining granules mixed in with the compost prior to planting have proved particularly effective in the mangers.

'We used to liquid feed at the same time, but now we tend to use slow-release fertiliser tablets pushed into the compost because this is less time-consuming. Actually I prefer liquid feeds as they have a more instant effect because you do not have to wait for them to break down. They also act as a foliar feed,' says Sam.

Unusual ways with containers

In the past Sam has experimented with a number of unconventional containers. This normally occurs when Tatton is

Hanging baskets arranged to form a pillar of growth.

used as a venue for weddings and similar functions, or when special display gardens are produced in the grounds. Four ideas are described below:

● **Litter baskets (tall wire ones, flared out at the top, commonly seen in parks)**
These are lined with black polythene and gradually backfilled with compost as busy Lizzies are inserted through holes made in the plastic. Soon the liner becomes totally lost beneath luxuriant plant growth, creating a stunning floral column.

● **Arranging hanging baskets to create a pillar of growth**
'This is a most effective way of displaying plants because you end up with a pillar of flowers, but the important thing is to make sure the supporting bracket as well as all the hanging basket chains are exceptionally strong.' The uppermost basket is planted in the traditional way, with plants spilling out from the top as well as the sides. All the lower ones are planted with trailers only and are then attached to the basket immediately above to create a tumbling waterfall of flowers.

● **Chimney pots**
These come in a wide variety of designs and sizes, and look particularly effective when grouped together. Instead of filling their entire depth with compost and planting within that, Sam recommends choosing plants in appropriately sized plastic pots that fit snugly within the neck of the chimney pot. 'That way you can simply swap over the display as the mood takes you. As long as you have enough plants growing in the right sized pots, you can change things round overnight and really fool the neighbours!' he laughs.

● **Climbers in pots**
Rhodochiton atrosanguineus, a slender-stemmed climber with heart-shaped leaves and unusual, tubular, blackish-purple flowers, and the extremely vigorous golden hop, have both been used successfully as individual specimens in large containers. All they require is a wigwam of canes tied at the top for support.

Fibreglass liners

At Tatton the Italian urns on the Terrace are about 90cm (3ft) deep. This means a huge volume of compost is required to fill them, the greatest part of which will be untouched by the roots of annuals that never go down that far. To overcome this problem the containers are fitted with home-made fibreglass liners. These are easy, if a little messy, to create yourself, provided you make a form out of wire netting first. Both the inside and outside of the mould are covered with fibreglass matting over which resin is painted. Holes for drainage must be added while still wet. Sam also recommends making two hand-wide slits near the top to facilitate removing the liner from the container.

Tips

● Always replace the compost in your containers at the start of the growing season. The display will never give of its best if you cut corners with the initial preparation.

● Only plant strong, healthy stock that is growing vigorously, and is fully hardened off. Unless you have somewhere to keep them, avoid being seduced by garden centres tempting you to buy bedding plants before you can safely plant them out.

● At the start of each season check that brackets and fittings for hanging baskets are secure.

● Ascertain from the stable or farm owner whether the manure you are buying has come from animals treated with chemicals. Many of them will be harmless, but some may be detrimental to plant growth.

● When planting up containers in a courtyard or enclosed space, don't forget about fragrance. Heliotrope, bidens and scented-leaved pelargoniums will all add to the sensory experience.

Using climbers in pots:
Rhodochiton atrosanguineus
growing up a wigwam of
three bamboo canes in a
terracotta pot.

Calke Abbey

DERBYSHIRE

Area: 4 ha (10 acres)
Soil: acid, alkaline clay
Altitude: 91 m (300 ft)
Average rainfall: 635 mm (25 in)
Average winter climate: cold

Steve Biggins, with one assistant, concentrates most of his horticultural energies on the three walled gardens at Calke – Lady Crewe's Garden, the Physic Garden and the Upper Kitchen Garden – concealed away from the house. Restoring these late eighteenth-century gardens to their former glory has been a learning curve for Steve, who came to Calke in 1987, following a seven-year spell at Ickworth in Suffolk. 'The Trust took on Calke Abbey precisely because it was an icon of the country house in decline. In restoring it, we have to be loyal to the house and garden we found in 1985, to ensure it continues to reflect the eccentricities of the Harpur Crewe family. The last thing the Trust wants to do is to start rationalising the restoration and make it all spick and span,' says Steve.

Auriculas

Auriculas are members of the primula family, and are all derived from hybrids between two alpine plants, *Primula auricula* and *P. hirsuta*. They probably arrived in Britain during the sixteenth century with Flemish weavers and Huguenot craftsmen who were fleeing from religious persecution in their own countries. A century later, they were grown as Florists' Flowers along with laced polyanthus, hyacinths, anemones, tulips, ranunculus and carnations. Unlike most of the other plants cultivated at that time, they were grown purely for their beauty rather than for any intrinsic medicinal or culinary properties they may have possessed.

It is precisely because their flowers are so beautiful that over the centuries they have succeeded in generating the sort of emotion more often perceived in church than in the potting shed. This devotion in part explains why auriculas were gathered together in theatres, and shown off in pride of place on such an altar. On the purely practical side, these structures also afforded some protection from rain, which could spoil the powdery, white farina, or paste, of the blooms.

The auricula theatre at Calke

The auricula theatre at Calke probably dates back to the first half of the nineteenth century. Measuring about 5·2 × 2·6 × 1·5 m (17 × 8 × 5 ft), it spans the right angle where the north and west walls of the garden meet (see p.12). The bricked-in back lies parallel to its open façade. 'Because it is a wooden structure, its existence is very rare. Although I knew it was some sort of pot plant display from the remnants of staging that were left, it was John Sales, the Chief Gardens' Adviser to the Trust, who waxed lyrical about it because he recognised it immediately for what it was,' Steve recalls.

The brief given to the firm involved in restoring it was to recycle as much of the original timber as possible. 'Everything we do here, even in the garden, has to be sensitive to the fact that for many years Calke was in decline. Someone invoked the term "invisible mending", which means that all the repairs we carry out have to be of a high quality, but sometimes we have to camouflage the fact that they have been done at all. Therefore the auricula theatre ought not to look like a new one, but rather that we have arrested its decline,' he explains. Tiny scratchings of the original paintwork were used as the reference for the final stunning effect. The surround is painted a dull biscuit brown, while the shelves are glossed with bright blue – two colours from the original Calke livery.

The idea of having a theatre just for auriculas, which by their very nature only flower for about six weeks of the year, is quite an extravagant notion, even for the wealthy. Therefore it comes as no surprise to learn that garden records, scant though they may be, point to carnations having been displayed on the staging in vases as cut flowers to provide interest when the auriculas were removed.

Nowadays lack of facilities and resources, both human and financial, means that the National Trust has to take a more pragmatic approach. This is achieved by supplementing the auricula display with other plants. 'Being relatively new to the Trust, the garden has enjoyed a high profile, and the auricula theatre has played a part in that. However, we have also created a monster that we have to feed. The theatre has now become so well known that I must live up to our visitors' expectations by ensuring there is something for them to see throughout the open season.'

For this reason a wonderful psychedelic display of polyanthus in terracotta pots graces the theatre before the auriculas put on their act, while red, pink and white trailing pelargoniums wait patiently in the wings and prepare to take centre stage once their more refined, but fussy co-stars have bowed out. 'In fact, I think the polyanthus and pelargoniums look more stunning *en masse*, while the auriculas, because they are smaller with more intricate flowers, are best appreciated as individuals at close quarters,' says Steve.

Visitors' reaction to the auricula theatre has been unreservedly positive. 'People are fascinated that there is a piece of architecture relating to one kind of plant.' Keen gardeners in general and auricula fanciers in particular come for miles to see the 200 or so pots when they are at their best. Like all plants, the onset of flowering is affected by the weather, so visitors are recommended to phone the gardens, or 'auricula hotline', as Steve jokingly puts it, to avoid disappointment.

Cultivation of the Calke auriculas

Steve is the first to admit that he knew nothing about the cultivation of auriculas when a new collection was first put together at Calke. He did the best he could with the primitive facilities at his disposal, but it was only when Doug Lochhead and Val Woolley, two local growers with their own specialist primula, auricula and alpine nursery, introduced themselves that the future of the plants looked more certain.

Like many other enthusiasts, they saw the theatre when it was featured on television and came originally out of curiosity. 'After two hours talking to Steve, he suddenly said, "you've got the job", and we have been looking after them as volunteers ever since!' laughs Val. 'When we first saw them they were in fairly poor condition because they risked rotting off in winter and baking in summer in a very old, leaky glasshouse. For several years we continued to grow them at Calke, but eventually it was decided to bring them to our nursery where they are housed in their own poly tunnel,' she explains.

Val and Doug's brief is to put on the best show for the maximum time – usually from about mid-April to the end of May. 'Our aim is to build up a separate collection of auriculas for Calke based on as many different varieties and colours as possible. I reckon we'll have to grow about 1,000 plants to get 250 or so in flower at the same time,' says Doug. There are far too many cultivars to name, but three that put in a regular appearance at Calke are the crimson-red 'Argus', which dates back to 1897, the yellow and green fancy 'Hinton Fields' and the double, dark purple-blue 'Walton Heath'.

All the display auriculas are transferred from plastic to straight-sided terracotta pots before being brought to Calke, where they are lined out, in serried ranks, on the shelves in the theatre. Thereafter their maintenance – usually watering them and providing them with shade – falls mainly on Steve's shoulders, although Doug and Val will make the occasional visit to chart their progress and replace any plants that are past their best.

Propagation of auriculas

In common with most other plants, auriculas can be increased by seed or by vegetative means, which in this case is by cuttings or division of rooted offsets, often referred to as Irishman's cuttings. Since Doug and Val are trying to grow named cultivars for Calke, they will only use the latter method. Whichever propagation means you choose, follow their advice for sure-fire success:

Cuttings

Take cuttings only when it is cool because hot weather combined with too much water is likely to lead to rotting. As they are busy running a nursery, Doug and Val find September a convenient time; amateurs can attempt it any time between February and March, which precludes the need to overwinter cuttings.

● Using a sharp knife, remove the smaller outer rosettes with a short length of stem, often referred to as the carrot.

● Carefully remove any floppy lower leaves and insert the cuttings into a pot containing moist, gritty horticultural sand. Do not cover them.

● Keep in a cool, well-shaded spot, for example in a cold frame or a well-ventilated greenhouse until the cuttings have formed roots. Never let them dry out, but do not overwater!

Irishman's cuttings

Take these cuttings in September, or February to March, when it is cool, for the reasons outlined above.

● Carefully remove the parent from its pot and knock off the compost (**a**). Irishman's cuttings are side shoots that have already formed roots, and are generally easy to remove with a gentle tug, especially if they are near the bottom of the carrot.

● If the shoots appear higher up and have short, thick stems, remove them with a sharp knife or scalpel at the point where they join the parent (**b**). Dust all wounds with a fungicide containing sulphur.

● Pot up the cuttings using a gritty compost, and place in a cool, shaded position. Avoid overwatering.

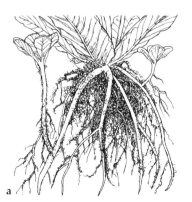 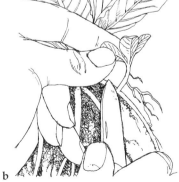

Taking Irishman's cuttings.   **a**   **b**

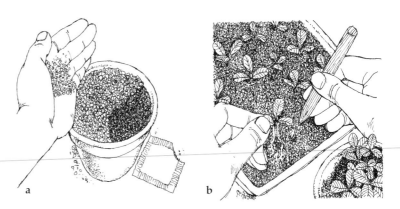

Sowing and pricking out auriculas.

a   b

Seed

To avoid overwintering susceptible seedlings, sow seed in early February as it benefits from a cool period to break dormancy. Germination can be sporadic, taking anything from four weeks for growth to appear. For more rapid germination, sow fresh seed in July as soon as it has been harvested.

● Fill a seed tray or pot with J. Arthur Bowers seed and potting compost, to which extra grit has been added for improved drainage. Firm in gently.

● Sow the seed evenly over the surface of the compost, then cover it with a very thin layer of sharp grit (**a**).

● Give the seeds a light sprinkling of water, then place the tray or pot in a cool, shaded spot until the seedlings emerge. 'The motto for auriculas is "sow 'em cool and grow 'em cool",' laughs Val.

● Prick out 28 seedlings to a full-size seed tray once they are large enough to handle (**b**).

● Leave the plants to flower in the seed tray. This way you need only pot up the most promising.

Where to grow auriculas

Auriculas are alpine plants, and as such are totally hardy. The nearer you can mimic their natural conditions, the happier they will be. Some, like the border and many of the alpine types, will thrive outside in the garden in a well-drained, partially shaded spot, but the show auriculas, which tend to be covered with a thick powdery white coating of farina, or paste, will only give of their best if protected from rain splash. This basically means growing them in pots in a well-ventilated alpine house or cold frame.

Compost and potting on

As long as the compost is well-drained, auriculas are surprisingly unfussy as to the type of container they grow in, or whether it is crocked or not, according to Val and Doug. The standard medium for most stages of their auriculas' growth is made up in the ratio of 1:1:1, using equal parts of J. Arthur Bowers seed and potting compost, John Innes No. 2 and 5 mm sharp grit.

As a rule of thumb, they repot their plants every September. This is not because they put on masses of growth – in fact auriculas do not like to be over-potted – but because it is a way of checking the roots and stem for signs of disease. Knocking off all the old soil and replacing it with fresh compost also helps keep the plant free of vine weevil grubs, one of the main scourges of the primula tribe.

Food and water

Excessive heat and cold combined with overwatering spells doom for auriculas because they become much more prone to fungal diseases, such as crown rot and root rot. In summer it is common for plants, particularly if they are receiving too much light, to show signs of stress, brought on by too much heat as opposed to lack of moisture at the roots. This is characterised by floppy outer leaves, which crisp up again once the sun goes down.

Remember auriculas store water in their stem and fleshy leaves, so as a rule of thumb only water when the crown, or centre, of the rosette feels slightly soft. Use a watering can and avoid getting any drops on the leaves. Plunging the pots in moist sand will help to maintain humidity levels, as will keeping a cool temperature in summer by opening all vents and doors, and applying shading to the greenhouse.

By nature auriculas do not have greedy appetites. However, flowering is improved if you apply a liquid fertiliser with a high potash content, for example Phostrogen, from the first week in March. Stop feeding once the buds show colour to avoid fleshy, cabbage-like growth which is susceptible to rot.

Pests and diseases

● General hygiene and good techniques will keep most diseases, such as crown rot and root rot, at bay. With the onset of autumn, auriculas naturally go into a resting phase, and in so doing many of their outer leaves shrivel and die. Remove these as they turn crisp to reduce scarring on the stem. If left on, they could get wet and attract grey mould, or *botrytis*.

● Val and Doug recommend placing the plants in a cool, north-facing spot in the garden for the summer months to toughen them up for winter. This will also go a long way in preventing red spider mite, which prefers the hot, dry conditions of the glasshouse.

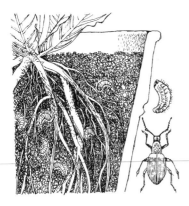

Vine weevil grubs around the roots of an auricula.

● Root aphids, characterised by clusters of woolly, white aphids on the roots and collar of the plant, are very difficult to control because of their protective waxy coating. A drench of systemic insecticide is usually the most effective way of eradicating them.

● The vine weevil larva, a milky-white, comma-shaped grub, is the auricula's most serious pest. It lives in the compost, and feeds on the roots and stem of the plant. Repotting with fresh compost in September will help dislodge both grubs and unhatched eggs. But the safest, surest way of eradicating them is to drench the soil with their biological control, a minute nematode which goes under various trade names, such as 'Biosafe', 'Nemasys' and 'Fightagrub'.

Recommended auricula cultivars

If you have never grown auriculas before, Val recommends the following to whet your appetite. All belong to the class known as alpine auriculas, and as such lack the farina, or paste, on the petals, making them particularly suitable for both indoor and outdoor cultivation.

'Argus' Crimson red with a white centre.

'C.W. Needham' Deep purple-blue with a light centre.

'Lisa' Purple-lavender with a light centre.

'Mrs L. Hearne' Grey-blue, shading out to a pale blue.

'Pippin' Rich pinky-red with a light centre.

'Sandwood Bay' Rich browny-red with a yellow centre.

'Sirius' Maroon and gold with a gold centre.

'Snooty Fox II' Orange-brown with a golden-orange centre.

Hanbury Hall

HEREFORD & WORCESTER

Area: 8 ha (20 acres)
Soil: neutral/clay
Altitude: 66 m (216 ft)
Average rainfall: 635 mm (25 in)
Average winter climate:
  moderate

From an early age, Neil Cook knew he wanted to be a gardener because he loved plants. With this in mind he applied to the National Trust when he left school, and was fortunate enough to be taken on as a trainee at Waddesdon Manor in Buckinghamshire before being promoted to Assistant Head Gardener there a few years later.

In 1988, he was appointed Gardener-in-Charge at Hanbury Hall near Droitwich, where he has spent the past five years implementing the restoration of the garden to its former eighteenth-century glory. The Trust was helped in this by a bird's-eye view engraving of 1732, a layout confirmed by a family portrait of owner Bowater Vernon in 1734, showing the garden in the background, and by recent archaeological excavations. So far, three principal features, the Sunken Parterre, Wilderness and Fruit Garden have been recreated. 'Although the reconstruction has been exciting, the biggest advantage is the opportunity it has given me to grow a greater range of plants. For me that is the most important part,' he admits.

Pots and containers at Hanbury

Although there are a number of permanently sited slate containers as well as stone urns, chiefly in the forecourt at Hanbury Hall, the majority of the pots used in the garden are made of terracotta, and are brought inside for the winter. 'We have a good range of different shapes and sizes of pot here, from lipped to beaker-shaped ones, from standard height to tall long-toms,' explains Neil. He estimates there are around a hundred containers to be moved each season, most of which are used to furnish the areas in and around the Parterre and Fruit Garden immediately adjacent to the house and long gallery. They are transported on the back of a tractor and trailer and are usually placed in matching pairs to flank a path or flight of steps.

'Although we do not have a precise record of what plants were used in the beds or pots, we do try to keep the planting as historically accurate as we can. For this reason we have chosen an initial cut-off date of around 1700, just before the house was completed, and only plants known to be in cultivation before that time tend to be used,' Neil explains. 'That said, it may be impossible to get hold of an old cultivar, so we opt for a modern equivalent which is more readily available. For example, we know marigolds were bedded out in those times, but the cultivar probably no longer exists, in which case we would choose a single form with a fairly loose habit to give the right impression.'

The other important criterion is its flowering season. A plant that will look good for several months is always pre-ferred to one that is short-lived simply because it extends the interest and enjoyment for garden visitors throughout the summer. White petunias are unbeatable in this respect, and Neil is also eager to try out cannas because he feels they, too, have great potential in pots. For historical accuracy only one species or cultivar is used in the same container; the modern idea of mixed plantings would not fit comfortably in a garden such as Hanbury.

Citrus collection at Hanbury Hall

Some distance from the main house is an attractive brick orangery, probably built around 1745. Although there is no record of citrus trees having been grown in it at that time, it is reasonable to assume this was the case. To help him set up and care for a collection of oranges and lemons at Hanbury, Neil was lucky enough to take part in a three-week exchange with an Italian garden to learn firsthand about citrus cultivation. 'At the moment my collection is new and small but my aim is to procure some historic cultivars from Villa Medici at Castello, which is near Florence, and to get budwood sent over for grafting in this country. I have now found a nursery willing to carry this out for me in the short term, but one day I hope to do it myself,' he says.

Compost for citrus trees

In the past Neil has always bought in a general John Innes No. 3 formulation and simply added one-third extra grit to increase drainage. This is particularly important for the winter months when citrus are more susceptible to root rot. However, following recent research in South Africa, he now intends to supplement some of the grit with coarse pine bark instead. 'Apparently the compost is less prone to compaction because the air spaces are retained for longer if bark is incor-porated. This is less of a concern for small specimens which are potted up frequently, but is an important consideration for large trees that are to remain in the same compost for years on end,' he explains.

Neil also has high hopes of a promising new product, comprised of pure composted bark. He feels this will not only provide an open, free-draining medium with the naturally low pH so beloved by oranges and lemons, but it will also make the pots much lighter to lift – a factor not to be scoffed at when about 40 citrus trees are constantly on the move.

Placing polystyrene crocks at the bottom of a container for drainage (**a**), and (**b**), carefully removing some of the old compost from a mature plant.

a   b

Potting on

Citrus trees have comparatively few roots for the amount of top growth they produce. For this reason they dislike growing in too large a container. Neil offers the following advice:

● When potting up smaller specimens, only increase the pot size by about 2·5 cm (1 in) at a time.

● Pot up in late spring to give the plant plenty of time to settle down and make new roots before the onset of winter.

● Ensure adequate drainage by using a good layer of broken crocks at the bottom of the pot. If the ultimate weight of the potted specimen is a major consideration, as it is at Hanbury, replace the crocks with large chunks of broken polystyrene instead (**a**).

● If you can, choose terracotta rather than plastic pots. Not only do they look better, but they will also be more porous, allowing better aeration around the roots.

● When a large 1·8–2·4-m (6–8-ft) specimen has reached its ultimate pot size, it can remain in the same tub almost indefinitely, as long as some of the compost is refreshed every two or three years. To do this, slide the root-ball from its container and peel away the bottom 15 cm (6 in) of old compost (**b**). If possible, carefully remove some from the top as well, but this will be more tricky as citrus tend to have surface roots. Pot the tree back into the same container using fresh compost.

● In Italy Neil discovered that all the citrus in pots were mulched with well-rotted manure. Not only does this keep the soil cool by reflecting the sunlight, but it also retains moisture at the roots. He will certainly try out this technique but suspects he may spend his time clearing up material thrown off by blackbirds.

Pruning

Citrus are best grown as bushes with round heads or as standards. Generally, little pruning is required other than

Snipping back vigorous citrus
shoots to maintain a rounded head.

pinching back vigorous shoots in spring to maintain a
rounded shape. A young specimen will grow far more quickly
if you sacrifice any fruit formed in the first few years.

Temperature

At Hanbury the citrus trees are moved outside only when all
danger of frost has passed, usually around mid- to late May,
and are brought back into the orangery in early September.
Neil tries to maintain a winter temperature of 10°C (50°F). If it
is any warmer, they grow too fast and if any colder, they do
not fruit successfully.

Feeding, watering and humidity

In summer Neil waters the smaller citrus plants on a daily
basis and floods the larger specimens once or twice a week.
The smaller the pot, the more regularly they need watering.
He also feeds the plants weekly with a specialist citrus
fertiliser. 'This is working out to be quite expensive, so we
may move towards using a much cheaper high nitrogen
fertiliser for the summer,' he admits. 'In winter we water
every six or eight weeks just to keep them ticking over. We
don't apply a winter fertiliser, even though it is recommended, because I like to keep them on the dry side to keep

The citrus in its pot on a round plastic plant tray, filled with pebbles or gravel to prevent the bottom of the pot from coming into contact with the water.

growth to a minimum. They are also better able to withstand lower temperatures,' he says.

Citrus plants like a humid atmosphere. Even in winter Neil regularly damps down the floor of the orangery on sunny days to maintain humidity levels. Another way of achieving the same end in the home would be to stand the individual pot on a tray or saucer containing pebbles or gravel, and keep the water level topped up to just below the bottom of the pot.

Common problems

'It is often quite tricky to diagnose what has gone wrong with your plant because the basic citrus reaction to anything is to turn yellow and drop its leaves,' laughs Neil. If the plant loses it foliage when you bring it indoors for winter, he offers the following causes and suggests possible solutions:

● too much heat.
Move the plant somewhere cooler.

● not enough humidity.
Stand the pot on a tray of damp pebbles.

● too dark.
Position the plant nearer the window.

If the leaves start to turn yellow, the cause is likely to be one of the following:

● iron or magnesium deficiency.
Citrus prefer a slightly acid soil. If the pH rises to above 6-6.5, the plant starts to suffer from a lack of trace elements, usually not because you have failed to supply enough, but because the roots are unable to absorb them. The solution is to apply flowers of sulphur, which reduces the pH of the soil to more acceptable levels.

● overwatering in winter.
Allow the compost to dry out thoroughly before you water the citrus again.

● nitrogen deficiency.
Apply a nitrogenous fertiliser to the plant throughout the summer months.

Recommended cultivars

Citrus limon **'Quatre Saisons'** Produces large blossoms and heavy crops of pointed lemons.

Citrus × *meyeri* **'Meyer'** A cross between a lemon and a mandarin, with small, juicy, thin-skinned orange fruit.

C. **'Ponderosa'** A cross between a lemon and a citron with large yellow fruit. Flowers and fruits from an early age.

Calamondin orange (× *Citrofortunella microcarpa*) A naturally dwarf and bushy hybrid. Everbearing (producing flowers and fruit continuously with little or no dormant period). Bright orange-red, bitter-tasting fruit.

Citrus sinensis 'Washington' A medium to large-fruited orange with sweet, juicy, virtually seedless flesh.

C. aurantium 'Seville' Produces the largest, best scented flowers, followed by slightly flattened Seville oranges. Can be grown successfully from a pip.

C. aurantium var. *myrtifolia* 'Chinotto' Bears very ornamental, myrtle-shaped foliage, and freely produces golf ball-sized, bright orange fruits.

Other exotics used at Hanbury

The orangery also provides a useful winter refuge for the following Mediterranean plants. All thrive in containers, and are placed on the gravel terrace outside the orangery in late May when all danger of frost is over. Neil grows them in a specially bought in John Innes No. 3 mix, where coir has replaced the peat part of the formulation. This is because the National Trust now recognises that in many locations peat should be regarded as a non-renewable resource. Part of current policy is therefore to minimise the use of peat in potting composts and to phase it out completely as suitable alternative materials and practices are found. To this custom-made compost he adds one-third extra grit for improved drainage. The plants are fed on a weekly basis using liquid Phostrogen, applied with a watering can.

● **Pomegranates** (*Punica granatum*) These are deciduous and bear funnel-shaped, bright red flowers throughout summer. Even better for containers is the more compact and rounded *P. granatum* var. *nana* which flowers particularly freely from a very early stage. This cultivar is easily raised from seed, sown with heat in spring.

● **Oleanders** (*Nerium oleander*) At Hanbury Neil grows the yellow-flowered 'Avalanche' and 'Sealy Pink'. In time oleanders can become large and top-heavy, but fortunately they respond well to hard pruning carried out in spring. Care should be taken to avoid the milky white sap as this can irritate the skin. They are also prone to scale insects. Neil has found that regular applications of soft soap keep the problem to a minimum.

● **Olives** (*Olea europaea*) These are positioned to flank the pair of wooden summerhouses overlooking the Fruit Garden, where their shiny glaucous foliage tones particularly well with the grey of the trelliswork. In hot summers they even bear fruit. Neil only prunes them when he has to because of their annoying habit of shooting out at right angles from the cut, making them lose their natural rounded outline.

Tips

● Don't treat watering as a chore. Use it as a good opportunity to look closely at the plants to check for signs of pests and diseases, to remove spent flowers, or simply to appreciate their innate beauty.

● Consider the cost of overwintering tender plants in a heated structure. By the time heating bills have been paid, it may work out cheaper to buy in fresh stock at the start of the growing season.

● Remember that even supposedly hardy shrubs can be susceptible to frost when planted in containers. Neil has given up growing gilded hollies for that very reason. 'Everyone assumes plants such as hollies are hardy, but we noticed they kept curling up their toes come the spring, not because the top growth had been affected by the cold, but because their roots had died,' he explains. If a prolonged freeze is forecast, lag the pot loosely with hessian and fill in the middle with an insulating layer of straw or bracken. Alternatively, plunge the pot in a sheltered corner of the garden until conditions improve.

● It is often better to replace plants rather than subject them to continual haircuts in a bid to keep them in scale with the container.

● Try growing highly scented plants to disguise undesirable smells. Neil recently found out that lemon verbena, *Aloysia triphylla* (syn. *Lippia citriodora*), was planted in the pots around the forecourt in former times to detract from the odour of sweaty horses!

Plunging an outdoor pot containing a holly bush into garden soil.

Overbecks

DEVON

Area: 2·4 ha (6 acres)
Soil: slightly alkaline
Altitude: 30 m (100 ft)
Average rainfall: 1,016 mm
  (40 in)
Average winter climate: mild

The man lucky enough to be in charge of Overbecks today is quietly spoken Devonian Tony Murdoch, who took over as Gardener-in-Charge in 1974. He came to the Trust having worked for six years at the Royal Horticultural Society's garden at Wisley in Surrey, where he looked after the Heather Garden. Tony subscribes to the doctrine, 'If you've got it, flaunt it', so rather than slaving to grow camellias and rhododendrons, standard signature plants of many West Country gardens with acid soil, he cashes in on the benign conditions and concentrates on colour, with the emphasis on bright annuals and tender perennials.

Pots and containers at Overbecks

Although there is a wealth of photographic proof to show that much statuary was employed in Otto Overbeck's time to heighten the Mediterranean atmosphere of the garden, none of it points to the use of any containers. This lack of hard evidence may bother garden purists, but the Trust prefers to take a more pragmatic approach and therefore uses strategically placed pots to enhance the tropical effect throughout the season for visitors today (see p.13).

For this reason Tony plants up five large, colour-themed earthenware containers opposite the conservatory, and places a number of smaller pots, each containing single specimens of *Agave americana* 'Variegata', on top of the pillars in the herbaceous garden. He offers the following practical tips for containers:

● The pots should always fit in with their surroundings. For example, at Overbecks they are positioned in pride of place on top of the walls, where they make dramatic silhouettes against the sky.

● The size and scale of the container should be proportionate to the plants it is holding.

● If you have the choice, err on the side of using large containers, especially in windy sites, where the added weight will help prevent them blowing over.

● Use tender perennials and annuals for the most sustained display of summer colour.

● Plant in loam-based composts such as the John Innes types, not only for the extra weight and stability that they provide, but also because rewetting them will then be much easier should they dry out.

Planting up the containers

The five colour-themed containers at Overbecks are quite shallow but very wide, and can hold a good number of plants. However, it takes two men to carry the containers, even when they are empty, so they are brought out of storage, crocked, filled with compost and planted up *in situ*, usually in early May. One tall or architectural plant, for instance a fuchsia, cordyline or phormium, will form the centrepiece of the display. This is followed by the next largest, for example three or four argyranthemums or verbenas. Finally, to provide the finishing touch, the sprawling and trailing plants are added around the edge of the pot; these are typically helichrysum, bidens or nasturtium.

Recipes for plant combinations

Like all good gardeners, Tony is not afraid to try out different plant associations. 'In fact I like to experiment and change things every year or so, otherwise they could become boring,' he says. He recommends the following combinations, all of which have worked well for him in the past. They are listed in descending order, starting with the centrepiece and working outwards. Bear in mind that the containers at Overbecks are large and can take many different cultivars; Tony advises you to moderate your own selection depending on the size and scale of your pots.

Scaevola aemula (fairy fan-flower)

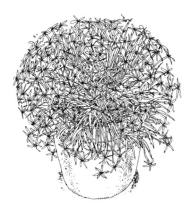

Solenopsis axillaris
(syn. *Isotoma axillaris*)

Blue and white theme

Argyranthemum frutescens
    or *A. foeniculaceum*
    (both white)
Felicia amelloïdes 'Santa Anita'
    (rich blue)
Salvia patens or *Heliotropium
    arborescens* 'Marine'
    (dark blue)
Convolvulus sabatius
    (pale blue)
Brachyscome 'Tinkerbell'
    (blue)
Osteospermum 'Whirligig'
    (white)
Scaevola aemula (blue)
Solenopsis axillaris
    (syn. *Isotoma axillaris*)
    (blue)
Pratia pedunculata
    (pale blue)

Yellow theme

Cordyline australis 'Albertii'
    (variegated foliage)
Argyranthemum
    'Jamaica Primrose' or
    A. callichrysum 'Prado'
    (both yellow, but 'Prado'
    is smaller)
Osteospermum 'Buttermilk'
    (golden)
Helichrysum petiolare
    'Limelight'
    (lime-yellow foliage)
Bidens ferulifolia
    (golden yellow)
Gazania 'Cream Beauty'
    (creamy white)
Tropaeolum majus
    'Hermine Grashoff'
    (orange)

A glazed urn with *Phormium* 'Maori Maiden' as the centrepiece surrounded by *Aeonium* 'Zwartkop' with *Uncinia rubra* around the outside.

Lotus berthelotii trailing down the sides of a container.

Red theme
Cordyline 'Purple Tower' (plum-purple foliage), red-leaved canna or *Fuchsia* 'Thalia' (reddish-orange)
Antirrhinum 'Night and Day' (crimson and white)
Verbena 'Huntsman' (scarlet)
Tropaeolum majus 'Empress of India' (scarlet flowers, bronze foliage)

Red foliage theme
Phormium 'Maori Maiden'
Aeonium 'Zwartkop'
Uncinia rubra

Crimson and pink theme
Cordyline australis 'Black Tower' (dark red foliage)
Argyranthemum 'Vancouver' or *A.* 'Petite Pink' (both pink, but latter is more compact)
Cosmos atrosanguineus (dark crimson)
Verbena 'Silver Anne' (pale pink)
Diascia rigescens (pink)
Brachyscome 'Purple Splendour' (purple-blue)

Silver and black foliage theme
Melianthus major
Astelia chathamica 'Silver Spear'
Ophiopogon planiscapus 'Nigrescens'

Indispensable foliage plants for pots and containers
Tony sets great store by the use of foliage in containers, not only to break up and soften large blocks of flower colour, but also to balance out the display. His top recommendations are (colour of foliage given first, followed by habit):

Lotus berthelotii (silver; trailing)
Lysimachia nummularia 'Aurea' (golden; trailing)
Helichrysum petiolare (grey; trailing and sprawling)
Helichrysum petiolare 'Limelight' (lime-yellow; trailing and sprawling)
Tropaeolum majus 'Alaska' (cream-splashed; bushy; red, orange or yellow flowers)
Senecio cineraria (felted, silver; bushy)

'Hostas and ornamental grasses such as carex also look good as single specimens in pots and are very useful for shady spots in the garden,' advises Tony.

Oranges and lemons at Overbecks
In 1991 a formal box and gravel parterre was created on one of the lower terraces at Overbecks. Viewed from above, it makes an eye-catching feature in what was previously an unappealing corner of the garden, and further enhances the illusion

of a Mediterranean plot, especially when five large citrus trees (a combination of lemons, *Citrus limon*, and oranges, *C. sinensis* 'Washington') take centre stage for the summer scene. A potent symbol of sunnier climes, they often display their ripe fruit, unripe fruit and heavenly-scented white blossom on one plant at the same time.

During the second week in May the trees are removed from their winter residence in the conservatory and installed in their summer quarters, where they remain until the second or third week of October. They are then returned to overwinter under cover in temperatures of no less than 7–10°C (45–50°F).

The logistics of transporting the trees, now about 2·4 m (8 ft) tall in pots measuring 60 × 54 cm (24 × 21 in), posed quite a problem on the narrow, steeply sloping paths until a local blacksmith devised the Overbecks tree transporter. Made of mild steel, the pot can be secured to the pivoting front section, and wheeled along by two 2·4-m (8-ft) long handlebars fixed above a pair of inflated wheelbarrow tyres. 'We used to put the plants on a hand truck, but they were still 60 cm (2 ft) off the ground. Because it pivots, the new transporter can be lowered to a few centimeters (1 in) above the path, which is particularly helpful when we come to the low archway in the garden,' Tony explains.

The Overbecks tree transporter.

Food and water

Many of the problems associated with citrus plants, namely yellowing foliage, boil down to incorrect watering and feeding. 'They need to be fed regularly, not just in summer but in winter too, surprisingly enough,' advises Tony. 'It is best to invest in two kinds of specialist citrus fertilisers, one for winter and another for summer, which contain the correct trace elements appropriate to the particular time of year.' He also recommends applying flowers of sulphur or sequestrene if the leaves become chlorotic (start to become yellow between the veins) because this is a sure sign that the plant is suffering from iron deficiency.

Allow the weather conditions to guide you when watering your plants. The soil should never dry out completely, but should not remain sodden either. As a rule of thumb, water about once a month in winter, about twice a week in summer. Avoid using hard water for misting or watering.

Propagation of citrus plants

Periodically Tony prunes his citrus plants to keep them in shape, using the snipped-off shoots as cuttings for new plants. He inserts 13-cm (5-in) long stem cuttings in a 50:50 silver sand and peat (or peat substitute) mixture, then places them, four or five to a pot, in a heated propagator to form roots. For those without sophisticated equipment, Tony recommends simply placing the pot in a clear plastic bag, which is tied loosely at the top, in a semi-shaded position. Taken in August or September, citrus cuttings root easily, usually within about six or seven weeks.

Plants grown from cuttings will be clones of the parent, displaying exactly the same characteristics. They will also start producing flowers and fruit within two years, although it is better to remove the fruit to allow the plant to mature. 'The question I get asked most by visitors is why their lemon and orange trees grown from pips have never produced any fruit. I tell them that citrus do grow easily from fresh pips, but the resultant plant is likely to take years to come into fruit, and may well not be worth waiting for anyway as it will probably be inferior to the parent plant. The exception to this rule is *Citrus aurantium*, or the Seville orange, which should start to produce blossom and worthwhile fruit after only three or four years,' explains Tony.

Pests and diseases

At Overbecks Tony chooses an integrated approach to pest control, which means he does use chemicals when absolutely necessary, but also employs biological means, in the form of natural predators and parasitic insects, to combat the problems. The main pests at Overbecks are listed below, with their biological control given in brackets:

- Whitefly (parasitic wasp, *Encarsia formosa*)
- Red spider mites (predatory mite, *Phytoseiulus persimilis*)
- Mealybugs (ladybirds, *Cryptolaemus montrouzieri*)

The chief drawback is that most predators require daytime temperatures of at least 15°C (60°F) and good light intensity to breed faster than their prey, so they are really only effective in the conservatory during the summer months. In winter when infestations build up, Tony sprays with a systemic insecticide, but must then wait at least six weeks before introducing biological controls because they are very sensitive to pesticide residues.

As soon as the plants, in particular the citrus trees, are placed outside, their general health improves and the pests are no longer considered a problem. If the leaves have become badly disfigured by sooty mould (a blackish powdery mould that lives on the sugary secretions produced by sap-sucking insects), Tony cleans them with plant wipes, an intensely laborious task but well worth the effort.

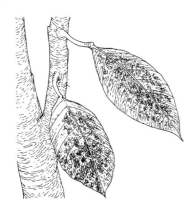
Sooty mould on citrus leaves.

Overwintering plants for use in containers

Tony does not have the luxury of much glasshouse space, so he must use what he has wisely. Most of the tender plants required for the containers and borders, such as *Mimulus aurantiacus*, argyranthemum, helichrysum, osteospermum, lotus and gazania, are overwintered as cuttings, taken when the summer displays are dismantled, usually in October.

The conservatory is also a useful refuge not only for the large citrus plants, but also for the agaves and cordylines, which can be tucked into any odd corner as long as they receive adequate light.

If any cuttings or plants do not make it through the winter, Tony is not unduly concerned because he can always buy what he needs at the many local nurseries he is lucky enough to have at his disposal.

Tips

● When buying plants, don't automatically head for garden centres alone. Why not try out your local nurseries, where you are far more likely to come across real gems that will make all the difference to your planting schemes? Fortunately for Tony, Devon is blessed with such establishments.

● If you live in a mild part of the country and your garden is overrun by helxine, or *Soleirolia soleirolii*, use it in place of sphagnum moss when planting up hanging baskets. At Overbecks it spreads at an alarming rate, growing all over paths, walls and borders, but its tiny, closely knit, bright green foliage does a fine job of disguising ugly wire baskets.

● Don't be afraid to try out different combinations. It takes a certain amount of vision to see how the plants will ultimately look together, but practice makes perfect. Try not to be put off if your early attempts do not match your expectations – you will get better at it. Inspiration can often be found in magazines, books and from visiting other people's gardens, so make a note of any plants or combinations you find attractive.

● If, like Tony, you do not want to take the risk with your containers by leaving them outside all winter, why not put them to good use and fill them with spring flowering bulbs such as tulips? These do not have to be planted until November, usually long after the summer display is over. They can either be placed in the conservatory, as at Overbecks, or grown on in an unheated greenhouse prior to being moved outside when they come into flower. Choose a flower colour that will complement your container. Tony uses yellow tulips in glazed, bronze-coloured pots.

Ickworth

SUFFOLK

Area: 28 ha (70 acres)
Soil: very alkaline/clay
Altitude: 76 m (250 ft)
Average rainfall: 533 mm (21 in)
Average winter climate: cold–
   very cold

When Ickworth was transferred to the Trust in 1956, 90 years of dense plant growth had obscured the crisp outline of the original nineteenth-century layout. Boundless enthusiasm and an ability to wield a chainsaw were prerequisites for anyone hoping to work in the garden, and Jan Michalak, at 26 the youngest Head Gardener within the Trust on his appointment in 1977, admirably fitted the bill.

After studying horticulture at Oaklands College near St Albans for three years, Jan became a student at the Royal Botanic Gardens, Edinburgh, but left after a year to take charge of an Edwardian garden in Perthshire. 'In fact this stood me in rather better stead to work for the National Trust because, unlike the other students at Edinburgh, I had the experience of actually running a garden,' he says.

Pots and containers at Ickworth

'The garden at Ickworth is a big con because we are trying to create an illusion of a Mediterranean garden using plants that we hope will be hardy in our climate. As in Italy, summers here are long and dry and our soil isn't terribly fertile, so we often get an authentic, parched look. But because our winters are cold, it is a matter of trial and error finding out what will survive,' he explains. 'In the 1820s when the garden was laid out, it was a flat, open site. Around the edge they planted yew and evergreen oak to act as a windbreak. Although the trees were totally hardy, they grew slowly until they were established. The trouble was the exotics, like the cypresses, were much more tender but put on about 90 cm (3 ft) of growth in one season. Obviously they raced away, overtaking the plants which were meant to shelter them, until many were killed in the very harsh winters at the turn of the century. For the last 90 years the remaining plants were simply left to grow, and I am now reaping the benefits of all those mature trees and shrubs.'

Although much clearance and thinning were carried out in the early years of the restoration, Jan also replanted some of the more tender exotics, which could benefit from the protection the established species now afforded. These micro-climates have allowed many unusual plants to survive: pencil-slim Italian cypresses, *Cupressus sempervirens*, form silhouettes against the sky; *Azara lanceolata*, with its mustard-yellow, fragrant spring flowers, often assumed to be tender, is thriving, as are two olive trees which on occasion have even borne fruit. Not bad for a garden in one of the coldest parts of southern England.

'I used to try and plant at least one unusual thing every winter. It often pays off because we do not lose that much. John Sales, the Chief Gardens' Adviser to the Trust, says that I run the garden on faith. We take bets on what will survive, and he is often surprised!'

The same philosophy of deception applies to the plants in the containers. None of them hold seasonal bedding displays; instead they are all permanent subjects, chosen to trick the visitor into thinking they are more tender and exotic than they really are. Such arch-deceivers include the many tubs of *Agapanthus praecox* subsp. *praecox* (syn. *A. umbellatus*), which only require a modicum of winter protection provided by the unheated conservatory, in front of which they are placed for the summer months (see p.14). The blue African lily, as it is commonly known, has wide, strap-shaped, bright green leaves and large spherical heads of trumpet-shaped, intense blue flowers, appearing in late summer. 'We place them out on the steps because old photographs show it is a tradition long since practised at Ickworth. But I also see them as a break from the imposing architecture of the house,' says Jan.

Similarly the twelve Portuguese laurels, which are growing in large oak boxes as tall, neat evergreen pillars, provide visual relief from the stuccoed, biscuit-coloured north front of the building. Now fifteen years old and scarcely turning a hair in cold weather, they replace the bay trees which were historically grown there, but in Jan's words must have been 'blitzed away' nearly every winter.

Sedums, both the tall *S. spectabile* and small-leaved, creeping houseleeks, are used in the urns which line the gravel walk on the south side. They are colourful but understated and require very little maintenance other than an occasional water when bone dry, and cutting down in winter. Their other great asset is that they seem totally unaffected by the swirling wind which constantly licks round the rotunda.

The Orangery

One of the finest features at Ickworth is the conservatory, or orangery, located in the west pavilion. Because of spiralling costs, it was decided not to heat the building, but to grow plants in pots that would give the semblance of tropicality. Some, such as *Eryngium agavifolium*, with its spiny, sword-like rosette of leaves, and the dark green *Fatsia japonica*, with its handsome, polished foliage, would actually be hardy outside in most districts. Others, for example the evergreen, ivy-like × *Fatshedera lizei*, the glossy *Pseudopanax arboreus*,

Eryngium agavifolium

Fatsia japonica

with its hand-shaped foliage, and the olive-green bamboo, *Himalayacalamus falconeri* (syn. *Arundinaria falconeri*), do require protection from the worst of the winter weather.

Cultivation of agapanthus in pots

Being a slightly tender cultivar, *Agapanthus praecox* subsp. *praecox* spends half the year, from November to the end of May, inside the orangery. Apart from the initial effort of placing the twenty or so pots, rank upon rank, either side of the steps leading up to the building, they are surprisingly undemanding plants. The following are Jan's tip on getting the best from them:

● Repot only when absolutely necessary, usually every four or five years as agapanthus produce most flowers when slightly pot-bound.

● To sustain the display, increase the pot size gradually; over-pot them and you will be rewarded merely with leaves at the expense of flowers.

● When the ultimate container size is reached, don't be afraid to take a spade to the fleshy rootstock (**a**). By his own admission Jan treats the plants roughly, 'I think people are rather surprised to see me hacking away at them,' he laughs. Discard the central heart of the plant and repot the outer portions only, crowding them into the same pot to induce flowering (**b**).

● Use a lightweight, peat-free compost when repotting. Jan uses one based on bark and farmyard waste, to which he adds a long-lasting, slow-release fertiliser to preclude the need for further feeding throughout the season.

● In the years when repotting is not undertaken, give the plants a boost by top-dressing with fresh compost and slow-release fertiliser.

● Cut off the spent flowerheads only when they start to detract from the display. Some years this happens soon after flowering; other years they continue to look rather starry and attractive long after the blooms have faded.

● Keep plants on the dry side throughout winter and remove old yellowing leaves as they die back. Even though *Agapanthus praecox* subsp. *praecox* is an evergreen species, the crown of the plant will look tatty until new growth erupts in spring. Increase the watering at this stage.

Portuguese laurels in containers

Prunus lusitanica, or Portuguese laurel, makes a first-class topiary plant for containers. It looks like bay and can be trained and clipped into the same shapes, but unlike its

Dividing the fleshy rootstock of an agapanthus and replanting the outer portions.

a

b

aromatic counterpart, it seems to withstand the vagaries of our climate.

As with all plants normally hardy in open ground, they become very much more susceptible to frost damage when placed in containers. 'During the winter of 1983-4 we recorded night-time temperatures of anything from –10°c to –20°c (–50°F to –70°F), but none of them died, so they must be pretty tough,' Jan declares.

● Feeding and watering is the crucial factor when cultivating plants of this scale. At 2·4-3m (8-10ft) tall, and growing in about one cubic metre (1·3yd) of soil, they are, in effect, bonsai specimens. Repotting is impossible, so to keep them healthy slow-release fertiliser pellets are inserted into the compost early in the season and supplemented with a monthly slurp of liquid feed.

● Where they are clipped back to the same shape every season, Portuguese laurels tend to build up spurs of old wood. These should be completely removed or thinned out with secateurs to allow the regeneration of new growth.

Ivies in pots

The value of ivies should not be underestimated, as they are some of the easiest and most effective plants to grow in containers. 'I'm rather keen on ivies, particularly their arborescent forms,' says Jan. At Ickworth he uses a shrubby version of 'Goldheart', which he spotted in a bouquet in the house. He managed to root it and it now features in four urns that flank a flight of steps at the end of west border. 'I think it makes a tremendous container plant.'

As the urns are small, the ivies are watered twice a week in summer. To kick-start them into growth, a base dressing is applied in early spring, followed by occasional liquid feeds. Any green shoots are chopped out periodically to allow the yellow variegated ones to fill in.

Plants that create a Mediterranean atmosphere

'I'm always on the look-out for plants that look "not British". West Country gardens often provide me with ideas because so many exotic-looking species, such as tree ferns, can be grown outside there. I then try to imagine how they will look in pots for the orangery,' says Jan.

Holidays to the Mediterranean are another obvious source of inspiration for Jan. They have also made him realise the importance of provenance when sourcing plants. For example, olive trees found growing in the mountains in Greece will differ markedly from those thriving near the coast, owing to their genetic make-up. Consequently, plants propagated from the former are far more likely to succeed in the average British climate than those that come from the latter because they will be hardier.

To create a Mediterranean or subtropical effect for containers, Jan recommends the following plants. Depending where you live in the country, you may need to provide winter shelter for them, although an unheated greenhouse, conservatory or other light place should suffice. All will tolerate a degree or two of frost provided the compost is kept on the dry side:

Lippia citriodora **(lemon verbena)** Bears strongly lemon-scented foliage and small insignificant flowers.

Chamaerops humilis **(European fan palm)** Has handsome, evergreen, fan-shaped leaves and tiny yellow flowers in dense panicles.

Convolvulus sabatius Trailing perennial with bindweed-like lavender-blue flowers from summer to early autumn.

Coronilla valentina **subsp.** *glauca* **'Variegata'** Has small, cream variegated foliage and fragrant, vetch-like, yellow flowers in early spring.

Eucomis **(pineapple lily)** Bulbous perennials, producing strap-shaped foliage and a dense spike of starry, whitish flowers surmounted by a small tuft of leaves, rather like a pineapple. *E. comosa* grows to about 90cm (36in) while the taller *E. pole-evansii* is even more stunning.

Grevillea rosmarinifolia Has needle-like foliage and spidery, pinkish-red flowers from late autumn to early summer. Avoid tapwater for watering; use rainwater instead.

Hydrangeas Mostly deciduous shrubs with rounded, pointed or flat heads of pink, white or blue flowers from mid- to late summer.

Lavenders Small, rounded sub-shrubs with aromatic, grey-green foliage and fragrant, pink, mauve or purple flowers in late summer.

Myrtus communis **(myrtle)** Evergreen shrub with small, glossy, aromatic, dark green leaves and creamy white flowers with conspicuous stamens.

Olea europaea **(olive)** Evergreen tree, developing a rounded head with grey-green leaves and edible green fruit.

Osteospermum Spreading sub-shrubs with daisy-like yellow, white or pink flowers throughout summer.

Trachycarpus fortunei **(Chusan palm)** Handsome fan-shaped, evergreen leaves above a thick trunk.

Clematis alpina cascading from a tall urn on a pedestal.

Tips

● Concentrate on cultivating plants you think you can grow rather than struggle to grow those you know will not survive, because of the climate, for example. The trick is to hunt down plants that *appear* exotic. Remember, practically anything will look good in containers.

● The container is very important to the success of the display. Save up and buy the one you want rather than making do with cheap imitations. If you want a big terracotta pot, buy it, don't settle for a plastic one, unless your aim is to conceal it.

● Even empty pots and containers look good as long as they are in a busy garden. You may never get round to it, but it looks as though you *intend* to plant them up.

● If your aim is to trick people into believing what you have in your pots is exotic, avoid filling them with the same species that already thrive in your garden. At Ickworth, for instance, phormiums and yuccas flourish in the borders, so Jan is careful not to duplicate them in containers as well.

● Do not be afraid to experiment with plants in containers, because you can always remove them if they do not turn out as expected. Jan has found some clematis, such as the deep, rich red 'Niobe' or blue *C. alpina*, are as effective cascading down from the tall urns along the South Terrace as they are climbing up walls and fences. He is also very fond of sea campion, *Silene maritima*, which is planted permanently in the low vases in the Silver Garden. 'It is an ordinary, workaday sort of plant but it almost drips with white flowers in summer.'

Belton House

LINCOLNSHIRE

Area: 13·3 ha (33 acres)
Soil: neutral/sandy loam
Altitude: 52 m (170 ft)
Average rainfall: 686 mm (27 in)
Average winter climate: cold

Belton House and its grounds were given to the National Trust in 1984 by the present Lord Brownlow. Ten years later, in 1994, Fred Corrin, previously in charge of the gardens at Packwood House in Warwickshire, was appointed Head Gardener. He and his team of three are responsible for maintaining and manicuring the immaculate formal gardens at Belton. 'In many ways Packwood and Belton are quite similar because both have fine topiary specimens. But this garden also boasts a number of containers, which gives me the chance to experiment with plants,' he says.

Pots and containers at Belton

Ornamental marble and stone urns are the containers principally employed at Belton. Flanking steps or raised up on plinths, where they act like exclamation marks standing out among low mounds of bedding, they are strategically placed to embellish both the formal sunken Italian Garden and the Dutch Garden. The bedding displays laid out in the parterres are changed twice a year, and although the planting does not have to be historically accurate, it must follow strict colour schemes, which were favoured by the former owners. Red, yellow and blue is the theme in the Italian Garden, while yellow, blue and white is the order of the day in the Dutch Garden. The contents of the urns usually mirror the planting in the beds that surround them.

For spring bedding, tulips are *de rigueur* simply because no other flower comes close to providing the same impact at that time of year. Fred does not always stick to the same combinations every year. In the past he has used the tall, yellow, lily-flowered 'West Point', which looks delightful rising up through a wave of forget-me-nots, as well as 'White Dream', whose glistening white, cup-shaped blooms work particularly well with brightly coloured spring-flowering pansies.

Wallflowers also provide unbeatable colour, but Fred is careful not to plant them in the same place every year because they are known to be prone to clubroot, a soil-borne disease, more prevalent on acid soil, which can remain in the ground for anything up to twenty years. This is less of a problem in containers because fresh compost is used at the start of each season, but it is a real concern in the borders at Belton. The summer display, which is set out in the last week of May or the first week in June, focuses on pelargoniums, heliotropes, helichrysum and dahlias.

In summer the Italian Garden is especially well endowed with container plants. For example, two enormous potted specimens of myrtle together with six large pots of *Agapanthus africanus* are wheeled out of their protected winter quarters to spend the warmer months on the steps just outside the orangery. As a focal point at the other end of the central axial path that runs the entire length of this part of the garden is an attractive stone structure known as the Lion Exedra. Its ten arched niches, each with built-in, waist-high plinths, provide the perfect backdrop for container plants.

Biological control

Step inside the protected world of the orangery at Belton and you can almost see the plants growing before your very eyes. Not only are these controlled conditions near perfect for a wide range of temperate species, including cestrum, solanum and datura, but they also provide the ideal breeding ground for a number of common pests such as whitefly, greenfly, mealybug and red spider mite. Because of their increased resistance to chemicals, Fred is now convinced that the only effective way of overcoming these pests is to resort to biological methods, which involves introducing their natural enemies as a means of controlling them. Chemical use is avoided in the glasshouses of the nursery as well as in the orangery. 'Not only is this beneficial in a display house where the public are encouraged to wander, but it is also an advantage for the Trust, which is keen to be at the forefront of protecting the environment,' says Fred.

All the biological controls are temperature sensitive, so there is little point in ordering them until the conditions are warm enough; Fred finds May a good time to start introducing them. The main pests at Belton are given below, followed by their relevant control, how they are supplied and the optimum temperatures required for them to be most effective:

● Red spider mite – fast moving, orange mite, *Phytoseiulus persimilis*, slightly larger than its prey. Supplied on bean leaves. Above 22°C (71°F).

● Whitefly – minute, parasitic, black and yellow wasp, *Encarsia formosa*. Supplied as parasitised scales. Above 21°C (70°F).

● Mealybug – black and orange predatory ladybird, *Cryptolaemus montrouzieri*. Supplied as adults. 20-26°C (68-80°F) and high humidity. As the orangery at Belton is open to visitors, it is not at all feasible to fix netting over doors and vents to prevent the predators escaping, as the textbooks often recommend. Instead Fred releases the ladybirds at night to give them time to settle in.

● Greenfly – *Aphidoletes aphidimyza*, a nocturnal predatory midge, whose orange grubs feed on the aphids. Supplied as pupae. 18°C (65°F).

● Scale insect – parasitic wasp, *Metaphycus helvolus*. Supplied as adults. 20-30°C (68-86°F).

● Vine weevil grubs – minute nematode predator, *Heterorhabditis*. Supplied as a powder or liquid concentrate held in a sponge to be watered onto open soil or compost in pots. Soil temperature above 14°C (56°F).

Since biological controls were adopted three years ago, they have proved highly effective. They are also much more user-friendly, as the gardeners need not don the regulation suits, masks, gloves and boots required by law to apply chemicals. In part, Fred attributes his success to regular monitoring of the plants. Other important points to bear in mind are:

● Be patient. Don't expect all the pests to disappear overnight, because it takes time for predators to outnumber their prey.

● Do not be tempted to apply insecticides once you have introduced biological control, as most will kill off beneficial insects as well as pests. If you need to use an insecticide during the winter months, make sure it is one with a short persistence, with active ingredients such as derris or pyrethrum. Fred has also found soft soap effective against aphids on susceptible plants such as *Solanum jasminoïdes*.

● Distribute the control evenly over infested plants, as some spread very slowly.

Dahlias in pots

For sheer flower power in late summer and early autumn, few plants surpass dahlias. Fred exploits them to the full in the bedding displays of the Italian Garden, where the tall scarlet 'Bishop of Llandaff' is planted in the parterres and the similar, though smaller and double, 'Madame Stappers' is used in the urns at the top of the terrace. Both are blessed with attractive glossy, bronze foliage.

Unlike 'Bishop of Llandaff', which is widely available in the trade, 'Madame Stappers' is particular to certain National Trust properties, notably Anglesey Abbey near Cambridge, and is rarely offered for sale. For this reason Fred prefers to overwinter his own dahlia plants and increase his stock from cuttings. His recommendations are given below:

● Wait until the first frost has blackened their foliage, usually around late October, before cutting back the stems to about 15cm (6in) and carefully digging up the tubers. Wherever possible, avoid damage to the fat, fleshy rootstock.

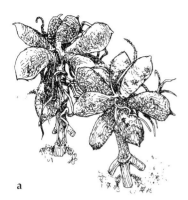

a

b

c

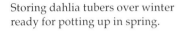

Storing dahlia tubers over winter ready for potting up in spring.

● Remove the bulk of the soil or compost, then set them upside-down to allow moisture to drain from their stems (**a**). Fred normally allows about three or four hours on a sunny, dry day for this procedure, but you can leave them for anything up to a week.

● When the stems have dried out, place the tubers the right way up in wooden boxes, label and store them, uncovered, in a frost-free place (**b**). 'Take care not to put them anywhere that will be too warm, otherwise the tubers are inclined to shrivel, especially on young plants. If this does happen, place the tubers in water for about twelve hours to swell them up again,' advises Fred.

● Bring out the stored tubers in late March or early April, and pot them up into large individual pots (**c**) or cover them with compost in their wooden boxes.

● Grow on and harden off the dahlias before planting them out into beds or containers during the last week in May or first week in June, depending on the weather.

Dahlia cuttings
● Bring out the stored dahlia tubers in early February, cover them with compost and place them in a heated greenhouse for forcing.

● Take cuttings when the young shoots have two or three pairs of leaves and are about 8-10cm (3-4in) long. Cuttings should be pulled away gently from the tuber so that a thin segment, known as a heel, comes away from the parent plant.

● Trim off the lower leaves, and insert the cuttings in a pot of moist cutting compost.

● Place the pot in a propagating unit with bottom heat, if you have one, or simply cover with a clear plastic bag to root. Wherever you put them, keep the cuttings moist and don't allow the foliage to dry out.

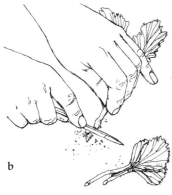

Propagating pelargoniums.

Pelargoniums

Given a sunny aspect, few plants will be so forgiving of neglect and still flower as freely as pelargoniums. This ability to laugh in the face of drought, together with the fact that they come in a wide range of colours, has made them particular favourites at Belton for the pots and urns.

To conform to the yellow, blue and red theme in the Italian Garden, Fred uses the upright 'Caroline Schmidt', an excellent old zonal pelargonium with double scarlet flowers and rather crinkled, creamy white margined foliage. It looks especially effective in association with the frothy yellow *Bidens ferulifolia* in the alcoves of the Lion Exhedra.

Pelargoniums also make a delightful addition to the former fountain head in the west courtyard (see p.16). Here the double red 'Brunii', a very prolific flowerer, is combined with the ivy-leaved cultivar, 'L'Elégante', whose trailing white and grey variegated foliage takes on attractive purplish-red tints if grown on the dry side.

Propagation of pelargoniums

Being tender, pelargoniums need to be overwintered in a frost-free place. Fred pots up a few mature ones to keep as stock plants, but prefers to start afresh each year with cuttings taken the previous August. 'The key to successful propagation is to use a good sharp instrument, such as a knife or pair of secateurs, because pelargoniums are particularly prone to die back if their tissues become damaged.'

● Select a healthy shoot about 8cm (3in) long, severing it just above a leaf joint on the parent plant (**a**).

● Remove all the lower leaves and trim the base of the cutting to just below the lowest leaf joint (**b**).

● Water the pot or tray containing the rooting medium, which is made up of equal parts of coir and perlite, and let it drain thoroughly before inserting the cuttings.

● Place the pot or tray in a light, warm position but not in full sun. Do not use a propagator or cover it with a plastic bag because the cuttings need a circulation of air around them to discourage grey mould or other damping-off diseases (**c**). If it becomes dry, water the compost from below.

● As soon as they have rooted, plant the cuttings into 8-cm (3-in) pots.

Tips

● Keep a few spare plants in the greenhouse or frame to use as replacements in the bedding schemes where individuals fail. This is particularly relevant if you garden on a windy or exposed site.

● Don't panic if frost is forecast after you have planted out your summer bedding in containers. Simply drape the plants loosely with newspaper or woven polypropylene fleece and remove it in the morning. However, if an overnight frost has taken you by surprise, get up as early as you can and spray the plants with a can of water. 'As long as you do this before the sun gets on them, the plants should escape the worst of the damage,' Fred explains.

● Compost in containers can easily become waterlogged, and since most plants hate to have their feet in constantly wet soil, adequate drainage is essential. Crocks, in the form of broken clay pots, are ideal, but if these are not available try stones or pieces of brick placed around, but not over, the drainage holes.

● Regular watering is paramount to the success of plants in containers as they are especially vulnerable to drying out. At the height of the season check the pots daily, and ensure you make provision for them when you go on holiday.

● Always choose the right compost to suit the plants you are trying to grow. Most will be happy in a general-purpose compost, but for lime-hating plants such as camellias, pieris and rhododendrons, you must use an ericaceous medium with a low pH.

Hardwick Hall

DERBYSHIRE

Area: 7 ha (17.5 acres)
Soil: alkaline/light sandy loam
Altitude: 178 m (584 ft)
Average rainfall: 660 mm (26 in)
Average winter climate:
    moderate to cold

The man responsible for the grounds at Hardwick Hall is Head Gardener Robin Allen, who came to Derbyshire in 1983, having studied at the Royal Botanic Garden, Edinburgh, before gaining experience in several private gardens. 'Even now, it never fails to surprise me how much sheer pleasure I get when I spend the whole day working in the garden. I also get a buzz from knowing that I am helping to steer the boat along the right course and that the garden team is happy,' he says in his characteristically careful and considered way. But like all gardeners, his greatest satisfaction comes from being able to grow a wide range of plants at Hardwick, 'for me that has to be the bottom line.'

Pots and containers at Hardwick

Unlike Powis Castle, where container plantings play a major role in the general scheme of things, Hardwick Hall is not generally known for its outdoor potted displays. In fact, if you blink, you might even miss them! I refer mainly to the two large wash coppers at the base of the south tower of the Hall; it is because they do such a fine job of brightening a potentially sterile spot that they warrant inclusion in this book. 'They are important because they furnish a very difficult area. You've got 100 ft (30 m) of building towering above you, bare flagstones beneath, and a pair of large yew hedges to the side. The containers certainly help to break up and soften those hard lines,' explains Robin.

When they were first put into position, they flanked a particularly decorative peacock bench. Unfortunately it has since been removed because it was felt that pieces of falling masonry could prove too hazardous for visitors sitting below. 'The trouble is the area now looks rather sparse. It is a problem we will have to address soon,' he says.

The need for security in the National Trust

The present coppers are replicas of the original pair which were stolen several years ago – an all too common fate for many garden statues and ornaments. Robin is still upset by the episode. 'They had just been potted up with summer bedding. Because of the exposed site I had been out there till nine o'clock in the evening staking and tying in the plants. A few weeks later we came in to find the contents had been tipped out and the coppers had been rolled away. We never did recover them.'

At first he tried obtaining second-hand ones, but found they were too badly damaged, so the Trust commissioned new replacements. Eventually Robin tracked down the supplier of a whisky distillery in Scotland, to whom he presented his own sketches and measurements for a pair of lipped, 66cm (26in) high, riveted wash coppers with a diameter of 86cm (34in). 'I was over the moon when I saw them. They are made of heavy grade copper and should still be around in a hundred years' time.' But Robin is taking no chances: they have been bolted, chained, padlocked and wired to the security system.

His only reservation is that, as yet, they have not adopted the blue-green patina of the originals. He would prefer them to age naturally, but suggestions to speed up the weathering process have included urinating on them, which he hastens to point out he has not tried, and spraying them with dilute vinegar, which he has done – without success.

Planting for the coppers

Robin admits himself that it often comes down to gut feeling when choosing the plants for the coppers. Although not hide-bound to use historically correct species and cultivars, he tries to avoid those he feels are too flamboyant or modern for Hardwick. For instance, one year he changed his mind about using the feathery *Argyranthemum gracile* 'Chelsea Girl' because he considered it too fashionable, too trendy.

Similarly, there are no colour restrictions, but Robin prefers a bold display that will not clash with the planting in the mixed borders either side. Two successful schemes that have shone out in the past are outlined below:

Orange and red theme	Blue and red theme

Fuchsia 'Thalia'
    Orange-scarlet flowers;
    upright; 45–90cm
    (18–36in) tall
	Salvia microphylla
	    Crimson flowers; upright;
	    90–120cm (3–4ft) tall

Pelargonium 'The Boar'
    Apricot-orange flowers;
    spreading; 50–60cm
    (20–24in) tall
	Lavandula pinnata
	    Blue-purple flowers;
	    grey-green foliage;
	    upright; 90cm (3ft) tall

Lotus berthelotii
    Reddish-orange flowers;
    long and trailing; 20cm
    (8in) tall
	Verbena 'Loveliness'
	    Mid-blue flowers;
	    spreading; 30cm (12in) tall

Although the garden is enclosed by walls, a great deal of turbulence is created by wind blowing around the Hall, so the chosen plants must be tough enough to withstand constant buffeting. For an exposed site he recommends:

● plants which by their nature tend to be shrubby, such as fuchsias, lavenders and argyranthemums. Their growth is fairly rigid and less prone to snapping off.

● plants that generally do not grow above 60cm (24in), such as antirrhinums, petunias and most verbenas.

● low, mound-forming perennials and alpines – violas, small campanulas and sedums – too small to be bothered by wind.

Spring bedding

The coppers are bedded out twice a year. Past spring displays have relied on tulips and forget-me-nots, or on polyanthus.

Polyanthus

Spring-flowering polyanthus in a copper urn.

The members of the primula family are a notoriously promiscuous lot, cross-pollinating with gay abandon, and often giving rise to seedlings with new or unusual colour and flower forms. At Hardwick Robin spotted one such polyanthus. 'It suddenly dawned on me after two or three years of having it at the nursery what a wonderful plant it was. It was definitely special and worth bulking up,' he says. He describes it as tangerine-yellow, darkening to orange-red, so producing a striking two-tone effect on one plant. 'I realised it would go very nicely against the colour of the coppers.'

Contrary to the usual recommendations of setting out spring bedding in autumn, Robin finds polyanthus perform equally well, if not better, in this exposed position when planted out in February. If you have a particularly good form of polyanthus you want to bulk up and use for bedding out, follow this advice:

● When flowering is over, usually around the end of April, dig up and divide the plant or plants. Only retain the young healthy offsets and discard the old, woody centres.

● Line out the offsets about 25cm (10in) apart in rows in a prepared nursery bed in a partially shaded site. Water in dry weather.

● In February carefully lift the plants to keep intact as much of the root-ball as possible.

● Space the plants about 23cm (9in) apart in the containers. When flowering is over, start the process again.

Forget-me-nots

These are one of the few bedding plants Robin grows from seed. His favourite cultivar is 'Indigo'. Forget-me-nots benefit

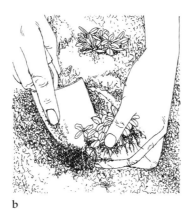

a   b   c

Sowing and transplanting
forget-me-nots.

from having a good root system to prevent them suffering
from mildew. As they are biennials, he finds the best method
for growing them is outside on a nursery bed:

● Sow thinly outside in a shallow seed drill at the end of May
or beginning of June (**a**). 'The shallow depth is important. In
one garden where I worked, they used to throw spent plants
from the borders in a spare part of the kitchen garden. There
they would remain for about a month to allow the seed to drop
onto the ground before being raked up. A patch thick with
forget-me-not seedlings would be the result.'

● When the seedlings are about 4 cm (1.5 in) tall, carefully dig
out and transplant them 15 cm (6 in) apart in small clumps, as
you would group small plants such as lobelia, for example (**b**).

● Allow the plants to grow on until October, then lift and
plant in their flowering position about 15 cm (6 in) apart (**c**).

Tulips

Like a happy marriage, certain plants belong together. Forget-
me-nots and tulips are one such combination. In the past
Robin has used the charming, broad-leaved species *Tulipa
marjoletii* to great effect. Growing to 35 cm (14 in) and flowering in May, it bears soft primrose-yellow blooms, shaded
rose-red on the outside. He has also been experimenting with
the much smaller *T. vvedenskyi* 'Tangerine Beauty', another
striking tulip, which in April produces its large, well-shaped
orange-red flowers with a yellow basal blotch. He intends
combining it with his coppery-orange polyanthus for a knock-
out spring display.

    After flowering, Robin does not discard the tulips. Instead
he digs them up and lines out the bulbs in a nursery bed to
allow the top growth to die down naturally, so building up
the bulbs' energy store for the following season. A useful tip is
to line the trench with woven netting, such as greenhouse

Lining a trench with netting before positioning the tulip bulbs.

shading material or an old onion bag, before setting the bulbs in position. This makes the task of retrieving them much easier, and ensures none are left behind.

Propagation

Robin uses the same basic method, outlined below, for propagating the tender perennials used in the containers at Hardwick. He recommends taking them any time from the end of July to the beginning of September:

● Using a pair of secateurs, remove healthy, vigorous shoots about 8cm (3in) long. These should be non-flowering, but if this proves impossible, nip out the flower-buds to prevent the cuttings' energy going towards flower production. However, to propagate *Lotus berthelotii* – often thought to be at best temperamental, at worst difficult – from cuttings, it is vital to select non-flowering shoots.

● For most plants, carefully cut off all but about three leaves from the shoot, and trim just below a leaf joint.

● Insert the cuttings round the edge of a pot filled with a coir-based compost, water thoroughly, then place in a closed case or propagating unit which has heated cables for faster rooting.

● When the cuttings have formed roots, pot up into a loam-based compost, to which coir has been added.

Tips

● If the weight of the finished container is an important factor, consider substituting broken polystyrene boxes in place of the usual crocks or broken bricks for drainage.

● Ensure you have bushy plants for setting out in summer by periodically nipping out the growing tips at a young stage.

● To avoid rooted cuttings and young plants becoming leggy and drawn in winter, try to slow down growth as much as possible. This can be accomplished by making them fight for water, so keep them on the dry side. Also try to maintain a constant temperature of 1°C (34°F), which is cool enough to discourage the plants from breaking into growth.

● Success with plants in containers is more or less assured if you do your homework at the design stage. Select the right plants, not only to ensure they are compatible in terms of their growing conditions, but suitable also from an aesthetic point of view. Before planting, gather them together and arrange them on the ground first. This is particularly advisable where different shades of the same colour are to be grouped together. Don't forget to consider foliage because this, and not flower colour, may often be the sticking point.

Plant Directory

Plants for a sunny aspect

Agapanthus See page 70

Alonsoa warscewiczii **(mask flower)** A bushy red-stemmed perennial, more usually treated as an annual (above). Its lax, somewhat trailing habit makes it ideal for hanging baskets and containers. Myriads of scarlet flowers are freely produced from June to October.

Antirrhinum majus **(snapdragon)** Strictly a short-lived perennial, but usually treated as an annual. The two-lipped flowers, borne throughout summer and into autumn, come in a range of colours, from white, yellow and bronze, to purple, pink and red, and there are bicolours as well. The best for pots and containers are smaller cultivars, growing 25-60cm (10-24in) tall. The Sonnet Series is bushy, free-flowering, tolerant of wet weather and comes in a range of shades. 'White Wonder' is pure white; 'Purple King' is magenta; and 'Black Prince' has deep crimson flowers set against bronze foliage: all three grow to 45cm (18in).

Argyranthemum Evergreen sub-shrubs with feathery foliage and masses of daisy-like flowers produced from late spring to autumn. As fillers for containers the smaller cultivars, such as the compact, yellow 'Cornish Gold', are recommended. Similarly sized with a height and spread of 60cm (24in), is the white *A. gracile* 'Chelsea Girl', which is grown primarily for its very fine, hair-like foliage. Smaller still, at 30cm (12in) tall, are 'Petite Pink' with abundant pale pink flowerheads, and 'Jamaica Snowstorm' with grey-green foliage and white daisy blooms.

Artemisia **'Powis Castle'** A clump-forming, woody-based perennial grown primarily for its fine, feathery, silver foliage, which makes the perfect foil for a wide spectrum of flowers (above). Annual propagation from cuttings ensures these otherwise vigorous plants remain neat and compact for use in large pots and containers.

Asteriscus maritimus A spreading tender perennial with small, silky grey leaves and golden, daisy-like flowers, produced from June to September. Growing to 45cm (18in), with a slightly pendulous habit, it is ideal for tall pots and hanging baskets.

Brachyscome iberidifolia **(swan river daisy)** A bushy or spreading annual with feathery grey-green foliage and masses of usually purplish-blue, but sometimes pink or white daisy-like flowers all summer long. Grows 30-45cm (12-18in) tall.

Campanula isophylla **(trailing bellflower)** A trailing tender perennial, more usually treated as an annual (above). Numerous saucer-shaped pale blue or white flowers appear on short trailing stems between June and September. The Kristal Hybrids produce larger, star-shaped blooms on compact plants and are best raised from seed sown under glass in late winter.

Citrus See page 56 and 64

Convolvulus sabatius Well-behaved trailing tender perennial producing a profusion of saucer-shaped lavender-blue flowers (above). More invasive, but equally suitable for large containers is *C. althaeoïdes*, its funnel-shaped, clear pink blooms studding the silvery-green foliage throughout summer.

Dahlia See page 76

Diascia A moderately hardy, mat-forming perennial (above). Their long flowering season and trailing habit make diascias valuable edging and filler plants for containers. *D. rigescens* has deep pink flowers on stiff, erect stems, 30cm (12in) tall. *D. vigilis* is hardier and even freer with its clear pink blooms.

Felicia amelloïdes (blue daisy) A rounded bushy sub-shrub, 30–60cm (12–24in) tall, with blue daisy-like, yellow-centred flowers. 'Santa Anita' has large, rich blue blooms, while 'Santa Anita Variegated' has white-splashed foliage.

Fuchsia See page 21 and 35

Gazania Low-growing evergreen tender perennials, best treated as annuals. Large, showy daisy-like flowers are produced throughout summer, and close in cool or dull weather. Cultivars in the Chansonette Series grow to 20cm (8in), and bear bright pink, bronze, orange, yellow or white flowers with a central darker zone. Those in the Mini Star Series are similar but more compact.

Glechoma hederacea 'Variegata' (variegated ground ivy) A hardy trailing evergreen perennial, grown mainly for its pale green, kidney-shaped leaves that are marbled with white (above). As a bonus it produces small, catmint-like mauve flowers in summer.

Helichrysum petiolare A tender evergreen shrub with woolly, silver foliage, indispensable in containers for its mound-forming and trailing habit. As an open-grown specimen it can spread up to 2m (6ft), and grow to about 50cm (20in) tall, but is considerably smaller in pots. 'Limelight' has bright lime-green leaves; 'Variegatum' has grey and cream variegated leaves.

Heliotropium arborescens (heliotrope, cherry pie) A bushy, short-lived shrub with wrinkled foliage, often grown as an annual. Its dense, often very sweetly scented flowerheads are produced throughout summer. 'Chatsworth' is vigorous, fragrant and bright purple; 'Marine' is compact and violet-blue; and 'Princess Marina' is compact, scented and deep violet-blue.

Lilium regale (regal lily) See page 29

Lobelia erinus A low-growing bushy or trailing perennial, more commonly treated as an annual and grown from seed. Masses of tiny blue, purple, pink or white flowers are produced all summer. Compact cultivars include 'Mrs Clibran' with brilliant blue, white-eyed flowers, or 'Crystal Palace' which has bronze foliage and deep blue blooms. Good trailing ones are the deep blue, white-eyed 'Sapphire' and purple-red 'Red Cascade'. *L. richardsonii* is a trailing evergreen perennial with white-throated, lilac-blue flowers. It is best propagated from cuttings.

Lotus berthelotii A tender, evergreen sub-shrub with long, trailing, silver foliage, and orange-red, lobster claw-like flowers, produced prolifically in long, hot summers. Its pendulous habit makes it ideal for hanging baskets or large containers.

Melianthus major (honey bush) A bushy, tender, evergreen shrub, with handsome, sharply-toothed, grey-green leaves and brownish-red flowers. Growing to about 1 m (3 ft), it is useful as a central feature plant in larger pots and containers.

Nemesia caerulea A spreading tender perennial, growing to 60 cm (24 in) tall, with two-lipped flowers, each with a yellow throat. 'Innocence' is white; 'Joan Wilder' is deep mauve; and 'Elliott's Variety' is light blue. Their flowering season extends from June right through to October if dead-headed regularly.

Osteospermum (African daisy) Colourful, long-flowering tender perennials, grown for their attractive daisy-like flowerheads, which are produced throughout summer and into autumn. Upright cultivars such as the primrose-yellow, bronze-eyed 'Buttermilk' are ideal as fillers in containers, but for planting around the edges, opt for trailing forms such as 'Tresco Purple' which has black-eyed, purplish-pink flowers, or 'Whirligig' with its unusual crimped, spoon-shaped, white petals and slate-blue eyes.

Pelargonium (geranium) See page 78

Petunia An extremely adaptable range of tender perennials and annuals, grown primarily for their showy flowers that are produced from late spring to the first frosts. The recently developed Surfinia Series, whose cultivars come in white, pinks, magenta, blue and red, are particularly useful in hanging baskets as they have an extremely vigorous, trailing habit and are tolerant of wet weather. However, they are only available as young plants, grown from softwood cuttings. Seed-raised cultivars are more numerous, and include the Carpet Series, which is very compact and spreading; the Duo Series, which features double blooms, often with darker veins; the Picotee Series, whose ruffled flowers are edged in white; and the Ultra Series, some of which will produce blooms with central white stars, creating a striped effect.

Plectranthus forsteri 'Marginatus' A trailing, tender, evergreen perennial, its pendulous stems easily measure 1 m (3 ft) in length. The bright green, nettle-like leaves are attractively edged with creamy white, and make an ideal foil for brightly-coloured flowers in hanging baskets or window boxes.

Scaevola aemula (fairy fan-flower) A trailing, tender, evergreen perennial with abundant, fan-shaped purple or blue flowers. 'Blue Wonder' has violet-blue blooms produced continuously from spring to autumn.

Tropaeolum majus (nasturtium) An easily grown, trailing and semi-trailing annual with rounded leaves and red, orange or yellow flowers with a prominent 'tail', produced throughout summer. 'Empress of India' is small and bushy with bronze-green foliage and velvety, crimson flowers; 'Peach Melba' is similarly sized with semi-double, pale yellow blooms and reddish centres; and 'Hermine Grashoff' has double, reddish-orange flowers, but can only be increased by stem-tip cuttings.

Verbena Spreading and bushy tender perennials, often treated as annuals, grown for their colourful, flattish flowerheads that are produced right through from summer to autumn. Seed-raised stock include the *V. × hybrida* cultivars such as 'Imagination' which has deep purple flowers and feathery foliage, and 'Peaches and Cream' whose pinkish-orange flowers fade to apricot and creamy yellow as they age. The Sandy Series is also recommended, with its erect and compact, magenta, purple, white or scarlet cultivars. More spreading in habit are the cardinal-red 'Lawrence Johnston', shell-pink 'Silver Anne' and magenta-pink 'Sissinghurst', all of which must be increased through cuttings.

Viola × wittrockiana (pansy) Small, bushy perennials, usually treated as annuals, with round, velvety, plain or bicoloured flowers, often with distinctive 'monkey' faces. Depending on the cultivar and when it is sown, you could have a succession of colour interest all year round. Recommended winter and early spring flowering forms are the Universal and the Ultima Series in a broad range of colours. Summer flowering cultivars are more numerous. The Crown Series is made up of cultivars with clear, uniformly coloured flowers, while the Joker Series produces strongly marked pansy faces.

Zauschneria californica (Californian fuchsia) A clump-forming, woody-based perennial, whose slightly spreading habit makes it an ideal filler in a large container. Its brilliant scarlet flowers are produced over a long period, usually from July until the first frosts. At 25 cm (10 in) tall with a 30 cm (12 in) spread, *Z. californica* subsp. *cana* 'Dublin' is slightly smaller and has intense bright red flowers.

Plants for a shady or partially shaded site

Admittedly, this aspect is not ideal for the majority of flowering plants in containers, but it is an all too common one, particularly in urban environments. Where possible, go for pale colours such as white or yellow that show up well in shade. The same goes for variegated foliage. When used judiciously, it has the effect of bringing light to a dark, gloomy area.

Acer palmatum (**Japanese maple**) A small deciduous tree grown for its shapely outline and attractive foliage. Numerous cultivars are available. Especially good ones for pots include the mound-forming 'Chitoseyama' with reddish green, deeply cut leaves that turn rich purple-red in autumn; 'Linearilobum' with long, slender, deeply cut green leaves, turning yellow in autumn; and the vase-shaped 'Red Pygmy' with dark red spring foliage, turning gold in autumn. All the Japanese maples appreciate protection from cold winds and late frosts.

Buxus sempervirens (**common box**) A rounded shrub or small tree. Their small glossy, evergreen leaves and ability to withstand clipping makes them ideal topiary specimens. 'Suffruticosa' is probably the best for containers, being compact and slow-growing. 'Elegantissima' has narrow, white-margined foliage; and 'Latifolia Maculata' has yellow young leaves that turn greener with age. For best results, water and feed regularly, and clip in July or August.

Camellia A choice, evergreen shrub, with glossy dark green foliage and flowers that appear from winter to late spring. The hardiest and best camellias for containers are the *C. japonica* cultivars such as the semi-double red 'Adolphe Audusson' or semi-double white 'Doctor Tinsley', together with the *C. × williamsii* hybrids. 'Donation' has large, semi-double pink blooms; 'J.C. Williams' is blessed with single pale pink flowers; while 'Water Lily' has double, deep rose-pink flowers. Plant all camellias in ericaceous compost and avoid positions prone to early morning sun and cold winds.

green striped leaves that become red-flushed in autumn (above). Its mound-forming habit is best appreciated when grown as a single specimen in a fairly low pot. Position in partial shade for the most intense leaf colour.

Hosta (**plantain lily**) Versatile, clump-forming perennials, grown mainly for their beautiful bold, heart-shaped leaves. Their mound-forming habit and architectural foliage make them ideal single specimens for pots. Leaf forms and eventual heights vary, so your choice of hosta will probably depend on the size of container it is destined to fill. For large ones try 'Francee' which grows to 55cm (22in) tall and has puckered, olive-green leaves with white margins, or 'Royal Standard', 60cm (24in) tall, with ribbed, glossy, bright pale green leaves. Recommended medium-sized hostas include the steely-blue 'Halcyon', 35-40cm (14-16in) tall, with smooth, heart-shaped leaves; *H. lancifolia* with narrow, glossy, dark green foliage; and 'Wide Brim' whose puckered, dark green leaves are conspicuously edged with a cream band. Where smaller cultivars are required, try the diminutive 'Blue Moon', 10cm (4in) tall, with puckered, blue-green leaves, or the 25cm (10in) tall 'Ground Master' whose narrow green foliage is edged off-white. Keep hostas moist and shelter from drying winds.

Impatiens walleriana (**busy Lizzie**) A tender perennial, more usually treated as an annual, with brittle, almost succulent leaves and stems, and flattened flowerheads. Any cultivar in the Accent, Tempo or Super Elfin Series is good, all growing 20-25cm (8-10in) high, and ranging in colour from white, pink, violet and lavender blue, to orange, wine-red and crimson. Excellent in partial shade as well as in full sun.

Hakonechloa macra '**Aureola**' Graceful, late summer flowering perennial grass with arching gold and

Lysimachia congestiflora A neat, pendulous perennial, trailing to 60cm (24in), with heart-shaped green leaves and clusters of golden flowers from July to September (above). 'Outback Sunset' has gold

and green variegated foliage and its close relation *L. nummularia* 'Aurea', golden creeping Jenny, is a vigorous evergreen perennial which also makes a useful edging plant for containers in a partially shaded site.

Nicotiana (tobacco plant) Short-lived perennials, best treated as annuals, bearing spikes of large flat flowers with long tubes. Older cultivars are often scented, though this attribute is largely lacking in more modern forms. Cultivars in the Merlin Series are short, about 23-30cm (9-12in), and therefore ideal for containers. The Starship Series show good all-weather tolerance. All have white, pink, red or lime-green flowers.

Rhododendron A huge genus of evergreen and deciduous trees and shrubs with spectacular flowers. There are literally hundreds of species and hybrids available, all requiring lime-free soil. The best for large pots and containers are those with naturally compact habits of growth, such as *R. yakushimanum*, with dark pink flowers that fade to pale pink or white in May or June. As an added bonus the glossy, dark green leaves have attractively felted undersides, which are especially conspicuous on young foliage. The Japanese rhododendrons, more commonly known as azaleas, are also excellent in containers, as they are compact with spreading, horizontal branches. 'Azuma-kagami' bears small trusses of bright pink flowers, 'Carmen' is dark red, 'Curlew' is bright yellow, 'Beethoven' is magenta-pink, and 'Kure-no-yuki' is pure white; all flower in mid- or late spring. Ericaceous compost, regular watering and partial shade are recipes for success with those mentioned above.

Plants for winter and spring colour

Auricula See page 48

Bellis perennis **(daisy)** A small rosette-forming perennial, with white, pink and red flowers from late winter to late spring. Cultivars in the Pomponette Series bear double flowerheads, 4cm (1in) across, and quilled petals. Grow in sun or partial shade, and dead-head regularly to avoid self-seeding.

Carex hachijoensis **'Evergold' (syn. *C. morrowii* 'Evergold')** A mound-forming, evergreen perennial grown mainly for its grassy, creamy yellow and green variegated foliage. Good in a mixed winter display or as a single specimen.

Erysimum cheiri **(wallflower)** A popular bushy biennial, with delightfully fragrant yellow, orange, red or mahogany blooms in May. Choose compact forms for containers as taller ones are more likely to

be damaged by wind. The Bedder Series produces short plants, 30cm (12in) tall, in vibrant yellow, orange and scarlet-red shades, while the similarly sized Fair Lady Series includes softer colours such as cream, pink and salmon.

Hedera helix **(common ivy)** An evergreen trailing perennial or self-clinging climber. Although the species is seldom cultivated, it has given rise to a number of attractive variants which are all useful in containers and hanging baskets when cascading over the side. Recommended cultivars include 'Eva', which has small, three-lobed, grey-green leaves and creamy white margins; 'Glacier' with silver-grey and cream variegation; 'Goldchild' which has broad yellow leaf margins; 'Ivalace' with glossy, dark green foliage that is crimped and curled at the edges; and 'White Knight', splashed with white towards the centre of the leaf.

Myosotis **(forget-me-not)** See page 82

Narcissus **(daffodil)** A winter, but more usually spring flowering bulb with yellow or white flowers. There are hundreds of cultivars to choose from, but probably the best for containers are the shorter growing ones, such as the creamy white 'Dove Wings', lemon-yellow 'Charity May' or golden-yellow 'February Gold', all 30cm (12in). Extend the flower interest into late spring by planting the strongly scented, multi-headed yellow *N. jonquilla* or the lemon-yellow 'Pipit'.

Polyanthus See page 40 and 82

Tulipa **(tulip)** See page 26 and 83

Vinca minor **(lesser periwinkle)** A prostrate, evergreen groundcover, its long, trailing shoots making it ideal for placing round the edge of pots and hanging baskets. 'Alba Variegata' has white flowers in mid-spring and leaves edged with yellow; 'Argenteovariegata' has light violet-blue blooms and creamy white-edged foliage; 'Azurea Flore Pleno' has double, light blue flowers; and 'Multiplex' has double, reddish-purple flowers. For best flowering, grow in full sun.

Plants that can withstand the occasional drying out

Agave Handsome, rosette-forming succulent plants with rigid, wickedly-spined foliage. Most species produce their funnel-shaped flowers and then die, leaving offsets to mature and flower in subsequent years. They require winter protection in most climates and are best grown as a single specimen. *A. americana* has grey-green foliage; *A. americana*

'Marginata' has yellow margined leaves; while *A.americana* 'Mediopicta' has a broad, central yellow stripe along each leaf.

Solenopsis axillaris (syn. *Isotoma axillaris*) A bushy, tender perennial about 30cm (12in) high, bearing myriads of star-like, pale to dark blue flowers from June to October.

Sphaeralcea munroana An upright or trailing perennial with finely cut, greyish-green leaves and saucer-shaped, dark salmon-pink flowers from mid- to late summer. Protect from winter wet, or better still overwinter as cuttings taken in spring or early summer.

Herbs in pots

Many of our most common culinary herbs are ideally suited to life in containers, and as they tend to have attractive foliage, they can make ornamental as well as useful garden features. For best effect either grow them individually in pots and group the containers together, or place a selection of your favourites in a large pot, taking care to choose ones that require similar conditions. Either way site them as near to the kitchen as possible for easy access.

For a sunny position

Bay (*Laurus nobilis*) A glossy, evergreen shrub that tolerates being clipped into attractive formal shapes. Good for adding height and structure in the centre of a pot.

Basil (*Ocimum basilicum*) A bushy annual, growing 20–45cm (8–18in) tall, with intensely aromatic, green leaves. More ornamental cultivars are 'Dark Opal', which has purple foliage and pink flowers, and 'Purple Ruffles' with its crimped and fringed purple leaves. Good as fillers in containers.

French tarragon (*Artemisia dracunculus*) A fairly tender perennial with small, aromatic, mid-green leaves. It grows 30–60cm (12–24in) tall. Take cuttings in late summer.

Oregano (*Origanum vulgare*) A woody-based perennial with upright and spreading stems bearing aromatic, oval, dark green leaves and pink flowers. 'Aureum' has golden foliage and is less spreading than the species, while 'Aureum Crispum' has curly, golden leaves and spreads more vigorously. Both are good as fillers or edging plants for containers.

Pot marjoram (*Origanum onites*) A small, semi-evergreen perennial, 30–60cm (12–24in) tall, with small, oval, bright green leaves and tubular white flowers in late summer.

Rosemary (*Rosmarinus officinalis*) A fairly hardy, evergreen shrub with aromatic, needle-shaped foliage and blue, white or pink flowers from early spring. For the centrepiece in large pots and containers try 'Miss Jessopp's Upright', which has a naturally fastigiate habit.

Sage (*Salvia officinalis*) A large, bushy, evergreen subshrub with aromatic, grey-green leaves and mauve flowers in midsummer. Attractive cultivars include 'Icterina' with yellow and green variegated foliage; 'Purpurascens' with purple foliage; and 'Tricolor', which is less hardy and has variegated cream leaves splashed with pink.

Thyme (*Thymus sp.*) Small bushy, creeping, evergreen subshrubs or perennials with tiny, aromatic leaves, and pink or purple flowers in summer. *T. × citriodorus* 'Bertram Anderson' has lemon-scented, yellowy-green foliage, while *T. × citriodorus* 'Aureus' has golden-yellow leaves. Equally ornamental is *T. vulgaris* 'Silver Posie' with white-margined foliage. All three are bushy, growing to 30cm (12in) tall, and would act as fillers or edging plants for large containers. Even better for spilling over the edge would be *T. serpyllum* which is very low and mat-forming.

For a cooler, partially shaded position

Chives (*Allium schoenoprasum*) A bulbous perennial with hollow, grass-like, dark green leaves, tasting of mild onions, and round, purplish-pink flowerheads in early summer.

Mint (*Mentha sp.*) A hardy perennial with highly aromatic oval leaves and pink flowers. *M. suaveolens*, or apple mint, has hairy, rounded, grey-green foliage, and is often considered the best for culinary purposes. *M. spicata*, or spearmint, has longer and more oval, bright green leaves. Both grow to 1m (3ft). Mint has invasive roots, so is best constrained in its own pot and then plunged into the general arrangement.

Parsley (*Petroselinum crispum*) A clump-forming biennial, 25–45cm (10–18in) high, with aromatic, curly or flat, bright green leaves. 'Afro' has tightly curled foliage, while *P. crispum* var. *neapolitanum*, or Italian parsley, has stronger tasting, flat leaves.

Gazetteer

Addresses

Belton House
Grantham, Lincolnshire NG32 2LS

Calke Abbey
Ticknall, Derbyshire DE73 1LE

Hanbury Hall
Droitwich, Hereford & Worcester WR9 7EA

Hardwick Hall
Doe Lea, Chesterfield, Derbyshire S44 5QJ

Hidcote Manor Garden
Hidcote Bartrim, nr Chipping Campden,
Gloucestershire GL55 6LR

Ickworth
The Rotunda, Horringer, Bury St Edmunds,
Suffolk IP29 5QE

Overbecks
Sharpitor, Salcombe, Devon TQ8 8LW

Powis Castle
Welshpool, Powys SY21 8RF

Tatton Park
Knutsford, Cheshire WA16 6QN

Tintinhull House Garden
Farm Street, Tintinhull, Yeovil, Somerset
BA22 9PZ

Additional National Trust gardens with container planting

Beningbrough Hall
Shipton-by-Beningbrough, York YO6 1DD

Cragside House
Rothbury, Morpeth, Northumberland NE65 7PX

Knightshayes Court
Bolham, Tiverton, Devon EX16 7RQ

Mount Stewart
Newtownards, Co. Down,
Northern Ireland BT22 2AD

Petworth House
Petworth, West Sussex GU28 0AE

Saltram
Plympton, Plymouth, Devon PL7 3UH

Shugborough Estate
Milford, Stafford ST17 0XB

Sissinghurst Castle Garden
Sissinghurst, Cranbrook, Kent TN17 2AB

Waddesdon Manor
Waddesdon, Aylesbury, Buckinghamshire
HP18 0JH

Gardening books from the National Trust

In the same series:

Climbers and Wall Plants: A Practical Guide
If the size of your garden dictates that the only way plants
can grow is upwards; if you want to keep your garden in
flower for the maximum length of time, then climbers and
wall plants are the answer. But how do you control such
gregarious plants; combat pests and diseases; renovate
a neglected fuchsia arch or grow an espaliered fruit tree?
Sue Spielberg talks to ten of the National Trust's Head
Gardeners to discover the secrets of their success with
climbers and wall plants.

More Practical Guides for 1999:

Gardening with Herbs
Gardening with Bulbs
More hints and tips from the professionals that you can't
afford to miss; Cathy Buchanan talks to the Head Gardeners
about their horticultural experiences with bulbs and herbs.

Gardens of the National Trust – Stephen Lacey
The ultimate armchair gardener's guide to the National
Trust's gardens from Acorn Bank, Cumbria, to the
Winkworth Arboretum in Surrey; from the re-created
seventeenth-century knot garden at Moseley Old Hall in
Staffordshire to the Arts and Crafts garden at Sissinghurst
Castle in Kent. Compare the formality of Hanbury Hall in
Hereford and Worcester with the quirkiness of Biddulph
Grange, Staffordshire, and the sheer exuberance of
Nymans in Sussex through the lavish illustrations that
accompany the text.

Gardening Tips from the National Trust
Seasonal hints and tips from National Trust gardeners –
from mulching to wildflower meadows, from pruning to
citrus fruit in pots.

The National Trust Gardens Handbook
A brief guide to 126 National Trust gardens with advice
on when to visit to catch their specialities at their best.

About the National Trust

The National Trust is Europe's leading conservation charity, looking after over 673,000 acres (272,000 ha) of countryside, 570 miles of coastline, 263 historic houses and 233 gardens and parks in England, Wales and Northern Ireland. The Trust always requires funds to meet its responsibility of maintaining all these properties for the benefit of the nation. To find out how you can help, please contact: The National Trust, 36 Queen Anne's Gate, London SW1H 9AS (0171 222 9251).

Membership
Joining the National Trust will give you free entry to properties and directly funds the Trust's work. For details of how to join, contact: The National Trust Membership Department, PO Box 39, Bromley, Kent BR1 1NH (0181 315 1111).

Legacies
Please consider leaving the Trust a legacy in your will. All legacies to the National Trust are used either for capital expenditure at existing properties or for the purchase or endowment of new property – not for administration. For more information contact: The Head of Legacies Unit, 36 Queen Anne's Gate, London SW1H 9AS (0171 222 9251).

The Royal Oak Foundation
This US not-for-profit membership organisation supports the National Trust's activities in areas of special interest to Americans. For membership and programme information in the US contact: The Royal Oak Foundation, 285 West Broadway, New York, NY 10013 USA (00 1 212 966 6565).

Index